MW01289784

Unlocking Key Biblical Words

BUCK ANDERSON
with
ABBY ANDERSON PERRY

…be a good servant of
Christ Jesus, constantly nourished
on the words of the faith…

1 Timothy 4:6

Unlocking Key Biblical Words
Copyright © 2019
by Buck Anderson and Abby Anderson Perry
All rights reserved.
ISBN: 9781719813686

Cover design by Michelle Aubrey

Special thanks to:
- Sally Coulson (editing)
- Valerie Anderson (Buck's photo; editing)
- Kathy Munnerlyn (editing)
- Britt Latz Photography (Abby's photo)

Feedback (typos, suggestions, etc.) welcome at buckanderson52@gmail.com

Purchase this book at www.amazon.com
Purchase this book at www.buckanderson.com
Free word studies aids at www.buckanderson.com

DEDICATIONS

To Val, my ezer, whose capacity for compassion and the well-being of others is unparalleled in my experience, and a wonder to behold.

—Buck Anderson

To Jared, my heart and my home, whose giving of himself helps me understand myself, know God, and love others more deeply.

—Abby Anderson Perry

CONTENTS

ACKNOWLEDGMENTS

I am deeply grateful to so many who have helped shape me:

- Dr. Allen Ross, who introduced me to the beautiful language of the Old Book at Dallas Seminary.
- Anita Carman, who encouraged me to write a book like this and helped create the title.
- Ross Munnerlyn, my cousin who left this life far too soon, but left behind a love for NT Greek to share with others.
- The faculty, staff, and students at College of Biblical Studies in Houston, Texas.
- The pastors, elders, staff, and congregation at Grace Bible Church in College Station, Texas.
- John, Erin, Emily, Riley, Gracie, Luke, Emily, and the whole tribe, thank you for being you and a blessing to me.
- My love to Val, Abby, Hillary, Olivia, Jared, Todd, Owen, Gabe, and "Little Selby Stonger, walking down the street!"

—*Buck Anderson*

Thank you to:

- Those who have taught me the craft of writing, especially Dr. Sandra Glahn and Jed Ostoich.
- My dear friends Macy English, Amy McGuffey, Andrea Poehl, Andrea Scott, and Liz Kilpatrick who see and name the gifts God has given me.
- The Slack Fam, my beloved writers' collective, who encourages me to live and write with courage and compassion.
- Mom, Dad, Hillary, Liv, Todd, and Selby, who stir affection in my heart for God's goodness.
- My greatest gifts—Jared, Owen, and Gabriel—who celebrate my work, fill my life with gladness, and delight in "our four family."

—*Abby Anderson Perry*

INTRODUCTION

As someone who came to know the Lord later in life (age 29), I (Buck) was not very familiar with church culture, especially the lingo used by Christians. Blessed with a powerful desire to explain God's Word to others, I was determined to "decode" the lingo by discovering the underlying concepts of key biblical words. Through the study of biblical Hebrew and Greek at Dallas Theological Seminary (1985-1989), the flame was ignited as I began to understand the richness of the key words God used to reveal Himself throughout Scripture. Since 1990, in Bible college classrooms, pastoral conferences, pulpits, church pulpits/classes, and personal discipleship, I have been on a quest to help others also see the rich stories told by these words. This quest has certainly marked my life and ministry and (hopefully) allowed others to appreciate the words of God more deeply.

When I teach a class of 5 or preach to a congregation of 1,000, I hold strongly to three principles. First, I am merely the servant of the audience, duty-bound to inspire learning and understanding of God's Word. Second, I am completely dependent on the Holy Spirit to truly illumine, convict, and comfort those in the audience. Third, I understand that 99% of those in the audience do not work in a church or parachurch organization and accordingly, are not immersed daily in Christian "lingo." **The third principle haunts me, frankly, as I'm concerned we might not be presenting God's Word to them in the most strategic way.** As I think through the makeup of an audience I imagine accountants, doctors, nurses, teachers, lawyers, plumbers, military, police, administrators, students, singles, couples, married, divorced, widows/widowers, all kinds of parents, teens, kids, Boomers, Generations X, Y, and Z, and all yet to come. They all spend the bulk of their day in various sub-cultures, marked by patterns of work and play, each with particular language and terms.

And you know what? Hardly any of them use the word "sin" at their job. Few regularly drops in "holy" in a sentence. "Faith" is often reduced to blind hope. "Grace" could be used to describe a fluid athlete or dancer. "Lovingkindness" is laughable. Some might include "righteous" in a sentence, but not many. So what do we do at church? We teach them a "gospel" that states all people have "sinned," fall short of God's "glory," and by "faith" one is "declared righteous" with God and then expected to grow in "holiness" and bring Him "praise."

At one level, we should be teaching folks about sin, holiness, faith, grace, glory, lovingkindness, righteousness, praise, etc. After all, these words appear throughout their Bibles. But more importantly, we must also walk the extra mile with them and explain the concepts, the underlying stories behind these precious words. The beauty of God's Word is He uses concepts and stories universally understood and practiced. The problem is the "Christian" words often get in the way. Everyone understands the biblical concept of sin; they just use other terms or labels for it. Ask the accountant to discover the error in the ledger. Ask the third-grade teacher to record the number of questions Johnny missed on the test. They'll both be able to perfectly articulate the concept that something is wrong or missing or not right. They'll both be able to explain sin exactly how God does in the Bible. They've become so familiar with the concept of sin they can explain it without using the term and in ways those in their worlds can easily understand. That's the "key" to Unlocking Key Biblical Words!

God uses certain key words over and over again in Scripture—sin, faith, righteous, save, grace, glory, holy, praise, etc. He selected them for a reason. He built the story of the Bible with them. These key biblical words are the notes of the song of Scripture. The key to a solid understanding of the Bible is this—words are the building blocks of Scripture, and wrapped around each of those blocks is a lock. By learning the universal concept found within each word, we will unlock them one by one. Once we gain a deeper understanding of Scripture's key building blocks, we can better understand God as He tells us Who He is and what He is doing.

So, let's set out on a journey to discover the clear, concise concepts of key biblical words. We'll go hunting for fresh ways of communicating ancient ideas. By first focusing on key Old Testament (OT) words (which we'll see carried over to the NT), we will become men and women of the whole book, and our depth of understanding of the OT will shine a magnificent light on our understanding of the NT.

We want us all to consider the stories behind these words. What's your story, Mr. Grace? What's your story, Miss Holy? Like a detective interviewing witnesses, I've interviewed each of these words in depth, developing a sense of their stories and uniqueness and will now share the findings with you plus help you learn how to perform word studies that will stick with you throughout your lifetime in the Scriptures!

The opportunity before us now is to approach these words as if they have layers of meaning, going deeper, deeper, deeper, as if the word has invited us to sit awhile and listen to its story. The beauty of doing a thorough word study is that the concept of each word will fix in your mind and become a gift that keeps on giving. Ready?

CHAPTER 1

HELPER
Ezer

Here I raise my Ebenezer,
Hither by Thy help I've come;
And I hope, by Thy good pleasure,
Safely to arrive at home.
Come Thou Fount of Every Blessing
Robert Robinson, 1735-90

Help me if you can, I'm feeling down
And I do appreciate you being 'round
Help me get my feet back on the ground
Won't you please, please help me?
Help!
The Beatles, 1965

Then the Lord God said,
"It is not good for the man to be alone;
I will make him a *helper* suitable for him."
Genesis 2:16

HELPER IS BY NO MEANS a dignified word in Western American culture, is it? The images it conjures up align quite perfectly, in fact, with my (Buck's) very first job. I kid you not, my title was "Helper." The tools of my trade were a broom, mop, and dustpan; the setting was a family-owned business located in a warehouse from which we sold wholesale air conditioners.

I wore a metal plated nametag on my shirt, displaying the word "Helper" for all to see. This was not an elevating position in the least. At its best and most hopeful, my role as "Helper" was the beginning of the way up to something better. The title communicated the idea that "helper" is the lowest ranking job there is, to be essentially without any authority, assisting only those in power.

Listen closely to the way I just described my first job as a "helper." **Please realize—this is not at all how Scripture uses the term**. In the Old Testament, the word for "helper" is *ezer* (or *'ezer*), from the *azar* word family. This is the suffix in the word "Eben*ezer*" we sing in Come Thou Fount or recall Charles Dickens' curmudgeonly character, Eben*ezer* Scrooge. In the context of Come Thou Fount, the hymn writer, in reference to 1 Samuel 7:12, "raises his Eben*ezer*"—his memorial stone of help—in tribute to God, the ultimate helper. The hymn, and even The Beatles' plea of "Help, I need somebody!" is more akin to the Scriptural usage of *ezer* than our typical Western notions of "helper."

A Word of Caution

Let's be careful not to approach the pursuit of understanding these key biblical words with a default position toward what can be called "English arrogance."

Because you and I are likely proficient in the English language, it is easy for us to believe we are therefore proficient in understanding language in general, and fully understanding what words mean on sight. There is not another belief more harmful as we seek to study Hebrew and Greek words—which by nature are intended to paint pictures and convey storied concepts—something English terms can often fail to do. So, with a little effort, let us be poets and seek to learn the rich deposits found throughout God's Word.

Helper Unveiled

As we unveil usages of the Hebrew word for "helper" in Scripture, I'll argue the Bible reveals a concept of the word "helper," which conveys the images of a shield, a deliverer, a rescuer, and a completer. Interestingly, the term shows up primarily in the context of war, such as a shield that assists in completing a needed defense. The term *ezer* often depicts a completed deliverance, a successful rescue.

In the Old Testament, the term *ezer* appears 21 times, 17 of those in Genesis, Exodus, Deuteronomy, and Psalms. In these 17 occurrences, an important discovery is revealed: only two persons are referred to as *ezer*—the woman of Genesis 2 and God! To be a helper is clearly, therefore, no small role, nor is it indicative of making a marginal contribution. It is a term by which God Himself is pleased to be known. *Ezer* is essential, and we're going to see how and why the concept and embodiment of *ezer* is so necessary as we begin to dig through the text.

Back to Genesis

As Julie Andrews sang in The Sound of Music, "Let's start at the very beginning, a very good place to start."

We see in Genesis 1:1-2, "In the beginning God created the heavens and the earth. The earth was formless and void, and darkness was over the surface of the deep, and the Spirit of God was moving over the surface of the waters."

These verses are likely very familiar to many of us. Whether they are or not, please join me as we go on a journey back to the beginning of the Bible and carefully observe its beauty. To go back to the beginning is a good thing; there's a great deal of treasure of beautiful concepts for us to extract from those early words of God found at the origin of the universe.

After studying Genesis for decades, I have come to hold the position the first chapter should be Genesis 1:1-2:3, because this section of Scripture covers all seven days of the creation narrative. From a literary standpoint, the most important verse in the entire chapter of Genesis 1 is verse 2, since it provides a framework—"the earth was formless and void"—for the activity seen in days 1-6. It seems logical the chapter should then conclude in 2:3 when the creation narrative ends with God's "rest" (*šābat*, from which we get "Sabbath" or "Shabbat") from His work of creation. This way, we have 1:1 serving as the topic sentence/headline of the entire narrative, 1:2 as the condition of the earth (formless and void) prior to (or at the start of) the six days of forming and filling activity (1:3-31), and then the Sabbath finale in 2:1-3.

Forming and Filling

If you and I were to form a vase from clay, we would mold it carefully, ensuring it could stand up securely and hold water. Once it was completed, we would put water and flowers in the vase, filling the form we had created in order to put it to use.

From where does this tendency we have to form and fill in our daily lives originate as we provide structure in our jobs, design homes to live in, fill bowls and plates with food, teach our children to draw an outline of a shape and then color it? The tendency comes from God, the Creator who formed the universe for the first three days and filled it for the following three.

When I worked in Houston, I had a meeting once a month that required me to drive past what is now NRG Stadium, home of the Houston Texans football organization. These regular meetings took place during the time the stadium was being built, and I can still see the construction process as though it was time-lapse photography. I have one mental snapshot of when the area was cleared, another of the construction fence being put up, yet another when the construction signs emerged, and so on. As the project began to unfold, it was like watching a huge erector set being played with by a (gigantic, I suppose) child.

The form of the arena was established before my very eyes as I passed by each month. But to what end? So it could be filled! Filled with people, filled with football games, rodeos, and concerts. Filled with seats, concessions, wins, losses, excitement, music, and applause. The arena would certainly exist when it was merely formed, but it would accomplish its full purpose only when filled. Just like at the beginning of creation, that which existed was given form that it may be filled.

After the six days of forming and filling, God rested, ceasing from His creative activity. God rests not because He is tired, but to celebrate His work. As created beings, we certainly do need rest because of tiredness, but we should also mirror God in our intentions as we observe grace-covered variations of the Sabbath, reflecting upon and celebrating that which God has done and that which we have done through His power.

Remember how I mentioned Genesis 1 should best end at Genesis 2:3? This is because Genesis 2:4-25 doesn't follow Genesis 1-2:3 chronologically. Rather, it provides more description and detail to something the first section already told us—the creation of man and woman. Genesis 2 is one of the most important chapters in the Bible. Its lessons are universal, its patterns instructive. Its characters (God, Adam and Eve) are prototypical and we can learn from their behavior.

Canyon Dwellers and Steven Spielberg

The Hopi Tribe of Native Americans formerly lived on the north face of the Grand Canyon in caves hundreds of feet below the rim. I would imagine if I were a filmmaker planning a film about the Hopi Tribe (along with Steven Spielberg, of course), I would begin with a storyboard. The board would show at the beginning of the film, the camera (along with Spielberg and me) would fly in from the south in a helicopter, hover over the expanse, and grandly reveal the entire north face of the canyon. The camera would then begin to focus on one small dark speck on the canyon wall, slowly getting closer and closer to it, until the audience could see movement, maybe a fire flicker, and then they might wonder, is that a person?

The camera would continue to zoom in on the movement and little flashes of fiery light until the audience could see—it's a family going about their day, cooking food, and staying warm by the fire we saw from a distance. The family clearly lives here, inside a cave on the north face of the Grand Canyon! The obvious question arises—how did they get there? The movie will then proceed to answer this question and tell the story of the

Hopi Tribe, dwellers of the Grand Canyon.

This is the same approach God takes as He "zooms in" on the man and woman beginning in Genesis 2:4. They are the family zoomed in upon amidst the grand creation of the garden. Where Genesis 1:1-2:3 gave us a 10,000-foot view of the people God created to inhabit His universe, the remainder of Genesis 2 zeroes in and observes the flicks of the fire and wonder of humanity.

Not Just Any Garden

First, God creates Adam from the dust of the "ground" (Hebrew *adamah*, from which "Adam" is derived), breathing into his nostrils the breath of life. God commissions Adam to keep and cultivate the garden He has planted in the East—Eden. Rather than your front yard flowerbeds or backyard tomato plants, picture a massive orchard, a huge grove of fruit trees, an orchard or vineyard like you might see in California or Florida. Adam's garden had a river running through it, every kind of beautiful fruit tree and two trees in the middle!

This is an enormous undertaking for one person, and given this, God considers it "not good" for Adam to be alone. Note it is because of the scope of Adam's work that God saw fit to provide a companion for him. It was not that God looked upon Adam and thought of him as insufficient as a person, requiring another to complete his humanity. Rather, He recognized help was needed for Adam to carry out his assigned task.

The first command given to Adam is about work—keep and cultivate the garden. The first problem arises—Adam's aloneness is deemed as not good—he cannot do this task alone. Yet even as God reveals the problem to Adam, He offers the solution—"I will make a *helper* (*ezer*) suitable for you."

God, the Drama King

If God were to have attended college, I think He would have double-majored in physics and drama. God loves to create, and He loves the drumroll—the careful building of momentum, the setting up of the big reveal. The drumroll He presents here is the sequence of His words and actions toward Adam as seen in Genesis 2:18, "It is not good for the man to be alone; I will make him a *helper* suitable for him."

God then brings all of the animals before Adam and observes as he names each of them, looking among their ranks for a potential mate. Adam naturally thinks he will find his helper in the animal world—where else would he find one?

"But, for Adam, there was not a *helper* suitable for him." (Genesis 2:20)

Heavenly drumroll, please.

The *Ezer*!

Remember the first thing the Scripture said was not good? Adam, alone, commissioned with a task too large. And now, here is this *Ezer*, a new person with a distinct purpose. She will come in and deliver, complete, and shield. Her existence brings about a new entity, so that the two "me's" become a "we," coming together to form something greater than each one individually.

Loneliness or Aloneness?

Genesis 2:18 reveals the situation Adam faced was not loneliness, but aloneness. This shows readers of Scripture that the reason to get married is not loneliness. Rather, the template God gives us for marriage is that it's a solution to an aloneness problem. A man is drawn to a task too big for himself, and he looks for a wife who will join him as a partner in completion of the task.

This is illustrated for us in Genesis 2:19-20 as the problem of Adam's aloneness is accentuated by the task of naming the animals. No sooner has Adam named them and been unable to find a suitable mate than the problem is solved by God as He causes Adam to fall asleep and takes blood, flesh, and bone from his side, creating the *Ezer* from them.

True Partnership

The *Ezer* is taken from Adam's side (Genesis 2:21-22), indicating equality and partnership. Their partnership is bigger than romance, it is oriented toward completion of the commission, their task at hand—keeping and cultivating the garden. Romance can certainly be a lovely part of marriage partnerships, but the structure, at the core, is a partnership toward a common goal, in which both partners provide needed input. If only one partner contributes, it's not really a partnership. To be a true partnership, both partners must be needed and critical to the completion of the task.

Adam is excited at the sight of the *Ezer*. The Hebrew text of Genesis 2:23a reveals he cannot even come up with a verb when he speaks of her. The man who had the vocabulary to name all of the animals can hardly put together a complete sentence as he beholds the wonder of this new creation now before him. But what he does say beautifully captures the heart of the introduction.

He exclaims, "This. Now. Bone of my bones and flesh of my flesh."

This—a new creature, like nothing Adam has ever seen.

Now—Adam had been looking for an equal, for a partner, yet had been unable to find one. There she is.

Bone of my bones—She is like me. She is what I need.

Adam's naming of the woman in Genesis 2:23b is a statement of empowerment and recognition of her dignity. "She shall be called *issah*, he says, for she was taken from *is*." The *ah* suffix seen in *issah* is added to denote a feminine noun in Hebrew. So, even the Hebrew wordplay used by Adam reveals the closeness of their partnership—*is'* and *issah*. Following suit, we see the same thing in English—*man* and *wo-man*.

One Flesh

In Genesis 2:24 God declares the man and woman to be "one flesh," a new term for the married couple. Note this status of "one flesh" is in existence all the time. Sex and romance are celebratory, the enjoyment of an existing status of "one flesh." Physical union is the celebration of the couple's status as one flesh, but the reality of one flesh exists just as fully outside of physical intimacy. What a beautiful and refreshing way to think about intimacy with one's spouse—it's actually a celebration of the union God has brought together!

Marriage, as we have seen in Genesis 2, is the precious union of a man and a woman toward a common task under God. The strength of the union greatly depends on an understanding of the human condition from God's perspective. Even before mankind's rebellion against God, He laid out work for Adam, work so large in scope he could not handle it alone, thus creating a keen awareness in Adam (and the readers of Genesis 2) of the need of a partner for him. A partner equal in capability and capacity to him; a partner desperately needed to complete the union, to create "one flesh." But partnerships only work well if both members are aware of their much-needed input into the arrangement.

For all men and women seeking to please God in a biblical marriage, we pray you will strive to honor the preciousness of your mates, appreciate their unique gifts and contribution, fulfill your roles as well and learn to embrace this revered creation of God—one flesh.

Is Marriage for Everyone?

It's natural to dig deeply into the rich concepts of biblical marriage in Genesis 2. However, we would be remiss if we allowed our readers to believe marriage is intended for everyone. Before the entrance of the *Ezer* in Genesis 2, Adam was a fully formed being—completely endowed with the image of God, lacking nothing pertaining to his personhood, his ability to relate to God and others, his capacity for love and spirituality. Adam's singleness (aloneness) was addressed only in relation to the enormous task (work) assigned to him by God. The *Ezer* was provided to Adam by God not to rectify something lacking in Adam personally (singleness) but to create a partnership powerful enough to keep and cultivate a huge garden as well as begin the task of populating the earth. But not all are called to such projects.

Several times in Scripture the virtues of the unmarried life is extolled. In Matthew 19, Jesus describes singleness as reserved for those "to whom it has been given." In 19:12, it seems He focuses on one aspect of the gift, viz., celibacy—either given at birth or through outside circumstances (injury, e.g.) or self-discipline "for the sake of the kingdom heaven."

The Apostle Paul views singleness positively in his first letter to the Corinthians. In 7:32-38, he cites several advantages/blessings of the single life. His goal is for his audience may be free from concern (7:32a). His motivation in writing is not to put restraint upon anyone but so the reader will benefit from his words. Next, in 7:32b-38, he sets forth advantages of the single life:

- Those who are unmarried are concerned about the things of the Lord, how they may please the Lord (7:32b).
- Conversely, those who are married have divided interests—their spouse, the Lord and the world (7:33-34a).
- Those who are unmarried can more easily concern themselves with the things of the Lord and how they can be holy both in body and spirit (7:34b).
- Those who are unmarried can more easily secure undistracted devotion to the Lord (7:35).

Clearly, the unmarried life has tremendous advantages for Christian service and personal piety. To view those who are unmarried as incomplete or lacking is not in keeping with the heart of God and the clear teaching of Scripture. **But Christian singleness, as well as Christian marriage, does not last forever.** All believers are part of the Body of Christ, a helpful metaphor designed to remind us of our unique and intimate relationship with the Lord and each other. But all believers also comprise the **Bride of Christ**. Each of us—male, female, currently single, divorced, widowed or married—each of us await a grand wedding ceremony. Each of us has one more wedding to attend. Not a wedding to observe as an invited guest but rather one in which we collectively participate as the Bride! "Let us rejoice and be glad and give the glory to Him, for the marriage of the Lamb has come and His bride has made herself ready." (Revelation 19:7). We are the Bride! We are **all** going to be married to the Lamb! There are so many things to do to be ready!

Searching for Ezers Elsewhere in the Bible

After noting the first usage of a key word in the Bible, we want to ask where else it is used and how. Remember this little maxim—the meaning of a word is determined by how it is used. We are now going to find out where else *ezer* appears in the OT, spend some time there, conduct an interview with *ezer* to see how it's used, and see what (or whom) the *ezer* really is. Some interviews may feel a bit bland, but every once in a while, a few will be profound, helping us create a robust understanding of the word. Hint: In the case of *ezer*, discovering **who** is the *ezer* elsewhere in Scripture is the key.

In Exodus 18:4, we see Moses' son Eli-*ezer*. In naming him, Moses states, "The God of my Father, was my *help*, and delivered me from the sword of Pharaoh."

So who is the helper here? God is. What kind of help did He bring? It was by rescuing His people from overwhelming oppression, by rescuing their very lives. In the context of likely death on a battlefield, the helper showed up. This usage of *ezer* illustrates beautifully for us the kind of help brought by an *ezer*.

Further military-type usages of *ezer* are seen in Deuteronomy 33:7, 26 and 29.

"…may You be a *help* against his adversaries."

"There is none like the God of Jeshurun,
Who rides the heavens to your *help*,
And through the skies in His majesty."

"Who is like you, a people saved by the Lord,
Who is the shield of your *help*
And the sword of your majesty!"

In each of these Deuteronomy 33 usages, God is the *ezer* who provides desperately needed help. It is a term of great nobility, dignity, purpose, and importance.

In Psalm 46, about which Martin Luther wrote the song *A Mighty Fortress is Our God*, God is described as the *help* of a refuge, a fort to which soldiers retreat from battle. We see here that to be the "help" is to be the safe place.

Similarly, in Psalm 146:5, we see the one whose *help* is the God of Jacob is "blessed"—he is secure because of the type of help God provides.

Psalm 124 is a Song of Ascent, sung and recited during trips to Jerusalem (to which the Israelites "ascended" to reach its lofty location) for the three great festivals of the Jewish calendar. In verse 8, David beautifully portrays the Lord as the *Ezer*-Creator, "Our *help* is in the name of the Lord, who made heaven and earth." The very One whose creative activity we discussed previously is also our *Ezer*, our ever-present shield and deliverer.

Wrapping Up

As we can see in just these few examples, Scripture is talking about a far more profound kind of help than doing menial tasks. These verses draw us toward a definition like that of a drowning man, his face breaking the surface of the water just long enough to cry, "HELP!" This is the kind of help depicted by the word *ezer*, the kind of help Adam needed in Genesis 2, the kind of help supplied only by a true and capable partner.

I greatly enjoy teaching word studies to those who enjoy thinking conceptually. It is a great gift when approaching the Scriptures, and one to be desired by all. Thinking conceptually can help us stop regurgitating the same old "church" lingo, and instead foster fresh synonyms and allow our understanding to expand...just as our idea of helper has expanded from sweeping the floors while others do the important work, to completing a defense, and being a valued partner in a grand endeavor.

For further study:

Psalm 20:2	Psalm 89:19	Psalm 146:5
Psalm 33:20	Psalm 115:9-11	
Psalm 70:5	Psalm 121:1-2	

CHAPTER 2

SIN
Chata | Hamartánō

Sin and despair,
like the sea waves cold,
threaten the soul
with infinite loss;
Grace Greater than Our Sin
Julia H. Johnston

Baby, can you tell me
Just where we fit in
I call it love
They call it living in sin
Is it you and me
Or just this world we live in
I say we're living on love;
They say we're living in sin.
Living in Sin
Bon Jovi

Wash me thoroughly from my iniquity,
And cleanse me from my sin.
Psalm 51:2

AS GENESIS 2 DRAWS TO A CLOSE, life on earth is wonderful. The world is beautiful, plants and animals contribute to the goodness, and a couple is peaceably governing the garden. What could possibly go wrong?

And yet, in just seven verses, all is ruined. Any student of literature would observe that the tragedy happens swiftly. We do not know how much time has gone by. It's not Moses' intention as the author to tell us. Rather, he writes to show how quickly perfection has turned to destruction. He leaves behind this idea—that which was beautifully and powerfully formed by God can be ruined swiftly by a poor understanding of God's words.

And so, sin quickly invades the world. We're going to meet this foe now, as revealed in the Bible. Sin is far more than moral failure or disobedience to God, though that's almost always how we use it. The Bible uses the word sin to talk about that which is morally lacking, but it also uses it to describe many other things that are "missing."

Let's Choose our Words Carefully

Consider the fact that 99.9% of people who sit in a church pew every week do not work at a church. They are doctors and lawyers and teachers and stay-at-home parents and marketers and accountants and farmers and store owners, and hardly any of them (perhaps none of them) use the word "sin" as a part of their professions. And yet, we have chosen to confine ourselves to the use of this word in our gospel and theological presentations, forcing an unnecessary vocabulary upon unfamiliar ears.

Why do we so often insist upon bringing our church words into the arenas of friends, co-workers, or audiences? God calls His people to discover concepts, images, and descriptions that will bring churchy ideas to life in non-churchy settings. We should not just speak a word and assume it can be understood. Rather, we should provide our listeners—whether we are teachers or parents or friends or speakers or pastors—with a concept around which they can fully wrap their minds and hearts.

Put it in the Trashcan

When I was a Bible professor, I would put a big trash can at the door of my classroom, point to it, and tell the students to toss all of their Christian lingo into the can. "Today we are going to learn how to talk to a construction guy at his place of work," I'd tell them, "He's a framer. He works with lumber. He measures boards and nails them together. He certainly understands the concept of sin; he just uses different terms for it. He's cut boards too long and too short. He's measured wrongly plenty of times. He understands there is a correct way to measure, frame and nail. He also understands that sometimes the standard is not met."

So, if our goal is to convey the biblical message to him and not just show him we know some Christian lingo, then let's use words and concepts he naturally understands, such as a **missing** header, a wall that **lacks** proper bracing, or a door frame that is **not** square.

Most everyone, Christian or not, understands the concept of sin. They just don't necessarily know the concept is called sin in Scripture. Or, if they are aware the word "sin" is used in Scripture, it's often shrouded in the mystery of a punitive God who is out to get people for ambiguous, deep, dark deeds. Certainly now more than ever, we need to keep these misunderstandings at the forefront of our minds and develop robust, compelling ways of illustrating terms rather than forcing people to adapt to our vocabulary and perhaps lose their respect.

A Basic Understanding of "Sin"

The primary Hebrew word for sin is *chata* (also *chata'* or *hata'*). The equivalent Greek word is *hamartánō*, from which we get the word "hamartiology," the theological study of sin. Each of us has a doctoral degree in hamartiology, by the way. We are very good at sin.

At its root, the word sin in the Bible means "to miss" or "to fail to meet the standard." So the question then becomes, what's the standard? As we look at the biblical text, we are far too quick to assume the standard is a moral one. Yet in our day-to-day lives, we are constantly pointing out that something is missing from a document, or the free throw shooter missed the basket, or our child colored outside of the lines. None of these examples are moral failures. The fact is Scripture uses the same word for many similar examples and more. To miss the mark or to fail to meet any standard is summed up in Scripture by the word sin. Therefore, sin must have definitions other than moral insufficiency.

Say you're at a baseball game. The batter hits an easy fly ball to the right fielder who drops the ball. The official scorer would call that "E9," which is an error on the right fielder. Imagine your surprise if the official scorer were to instead announce, "The right fielder sinned." "WHAT?" we would yell from the stands. "Sinned?! This ain't church! He just made an error in a baseball game!"

We would be right, but the official would be right too. The right fielder did not do anything morally wrong, but he did "sin" according to the biblical use of the word. How so? Simply because he did not meet the standard of catching the ball. The biblical idea of the word "sin" is exactly that. Let's begin to change our thinking as we look at various passages that use original words for sin.

There's Something Wrong with Everything

As you look around the world in which we live, it seems there's something wrong with everything. To illustrate, consider all the times in English where the prefix "mis" shows up. It's used routinely in our language. So when we are talking to someone unfamiliar with "church words," we can begin here, with common words that conjure up the idea of missing a mark, a standard unkept, things not as they were meant to be, perhaps morally, but often not.

Mistake	Misfile	Misfortune
Mislead	Mistreat	Misinformed
Misapply	Misplace	Amiss
Misjudge	Misappropriate	Misguided
Missing	Miscarriage	Misunderstand

Everyday Examples

I've found that a helpful way of grasping this idea of sin as it's explained biblically is this—imagine you own property along the San Andreas Fault and an earthquake occurs. Suddenly, there's a huge ditch in your backyard. The ground, which is supposed to be there, is not. It's missing. That is the picture, biblically, of sin.

Or you're driving along and suddenly your tire hits a pothole. "Come on!" you exclaim, "Somebody fix these streets!" What you're saying is, "Deal with that which is missing. Fill it up. Cover it over. Meet the standard of a road." That is the picture, biblically, of sin.

Or you're watching Olympic archery and a competitor's arrow misses the bulls-eye. The standard has been missed. That is the picture, biblically, of sin.

Or your child brings home a graded math worksheet with a few red lines on it. Your child did not morally fail by miscalculating 3+3. She just missed the mark, failed to meet the standard of providing the correct answer on the worksheet. That is the picture, biblically, of sin.

My grandson, Gabriel, was born with two mutations in one of his genes. These mutations have caused, among other things, missing muscle tissue and nerves in his feet. That which we would think of as supposed to be there is simply not. No one believes that Gabe is lacking in muscles and nerves because of a moral failing. It is simply that which is supposed to be there, is not there; it is missing. That is the picture, biblically, of sin.

Weeds result when something is missing in the soil or the plant. Cancer results when something is missing in cells. Baldness results when something is missing in hair follicles. Missing concrete causes potholes.

Even other cultures employ the term "sin" into their languages. The Spanish term *sin* means "without; lack of something," as in the expression "*sin* dinero" (without money; broke). Latin brings us "*sine* qua non" (without which there is nothing). Sin conveys the concept of missing, lack of, without, the failure to meet any standard.

Non Theological Examples

When studying a word in Scripture, I like to find what I refer to as "non-theological usages." The word "theology" means "words about God," and for us to understand the deeper meaning of words used in Scripture, we must also look at instances that show us how regular people in the Bible actually talked, thought, and acted. These usages are not found in contexts that focus primarily upon God (thus, non-theological), but rather focus on descriptions of everyday life and provide rich insights into their language.

For example, in Judges 20:16, 700 choice men are described as left-handed, each of whom could sling a stone at a hair and not *miss*. That word for "miss" (*chata*) is the same word that is used for Samson's sin, David's sin, and all kinds of other moral failings recorded in Scripture. Yet in this case, the word simply refers to whether or not someone can sling a stone precisely, nothing inherently moral about it.

In 2 Kings 18:14, Hezekiah king of Judah sends a message to the king of Assyria at Lachish, saying, "…I have done *wrong*…" Hezekiah is referring to the fact that he has not paid the King of Assyria on time, a payment of extortion, unfortunately. The "doing wrong" morally is the fact that Hezekiah was paying the Assyrians at all, rather than trusting God to protect the Israelites against those who would oppress them. But Hezekiah uses *chata* to describe his error of not paying on time.

This would be similar to my saying "my sin!," because I showed up 15 minutes late for a meeting with you. You would say, "Relax, bud. It's fine. You didn't sin. You're just late." But the Hebrew word *chata* encompasses all of these missings of the mark—lateness, a hole in the road, an overdue payment, a moral failing—all of it.

In Exodus 5:16, the Israelite foremen appeal to the Pharaoh who is ruling over them by saying, "There is no straw given to your servants, yet they keep saying to us, 'Make bricks!' And behold, your servants are being beaten; but it is the *fault* of your own people." The word for "fault" here is *chata*. The Israelites are saying to Pharaoh that being unable to make bricks without straw is not an error. Rather there is fault on the part of those who expect bricks to be made without straw.

In Isaiah 65:20, the prophet describes the future Millennial Kingdom and writes, "No longer will there be in it an infant who lives but a few days, or an old man who does not live out his days; for the youth will die at the age of one hundred and *the one who does not reach* the age of one hundred shall be thought accursed." The participial form of *chata* is rendered "The one who does not reach"—he is the non-reacher, the non-reaching one, the non-standard meeting one. It's not necessarily a case about a moral issue with the non-reacher. It's simply that the mark (reaching the age of one hundred years old) has been missed (by not reaching the age of one hundred years old).

Humpty Dumpty

Let's consider an example that many of us are familiar with from childhood—good ole Humpty Dumpty:

> Humpty Dumpty sat on a wall,
> Humpty Dumpty had a great fall.
> All the king's horses and all the king's men
> Couldn't put Humpty together again.

Hopefully, I am not the first one breaking this news to you, but Humpty Dumpty died. They could not put him back together again. He's broken in an essential way—pieces shattered all over the place with no mechanism for reassembling them into what they once were, much less breathing life back into those pieces.

We are no different than this—"prone to wander" as the hymn reminds. The shattered state of a world broken by sin is why we need a whole new order—not an order after Adam, but an order after Christ. Our participation in sin through Adam has made us unable to be put back together again, revealing our very nature as standard-missers who perpetually fall short, and thus we need a new way, a way that meets the standard on our behalf.

Poor Humpty Dumpty. He didn't make it. But our story has a happy ending. Through Jesus Christ we can be "put back together again"!

Theological Examples

Turning our eyes back to Scripture, we find many more uses of sin in the biblical text. In 1 Samuel 15:24-25, for example, Saul says to Samuel, "I have *sinned*; I have indeed transgressed…please pardon my *sin* and return with me, that I may worship the Lord." Saul is indeed talking about moral failure, but we can understand that failure more fully by drawing upon what we learned about the word *chata* in its non-theological uses. Saul is saying that he has missed the mark. He has crossed the line with God. He is asking the prophet to cover over what is lacking in him, filling the pothole in the road he is presenting to God, the pothole created by his sin.

Psalm 51:2, our key verse for this section, conjures a similar word picture. "Wash me thoroughly from my iniquity, and cleanse me from my *sin*," the poet David writes about his unlawful encounters with Bathsheba and Uriah. In asking God to wash and cleanse the sin, he is asking for his sin to be atoned or covered. He is asking God to provide that which is lacking in him to meet the standard.

We see many examples of the concept of sin in the New Testament as well. The words for sin remain conceptually the same throughout the New Testament because the writers of the New Testament were Jews well versed in the key theological terms and concepts first presented in the Old Testament. Thus, "sin" maintains the same concept in Romans as it did in Genesis. In Romans 3:23, Paul writes, "For all have *sinned* (*hamartánō*) and fall short of the glory of God." This illustrates the word picture that we saw in the Old Testament text, that of not meeting a standard. Paul adds another image for his Greek readers when he introduces the idea that those who have morally failed "fall short" of the glory of God. (See Chapter 6 for a thorough discussion of "glory.")

When we receive an Amber Alert, we immediately think, "The child needs to be found!" The concept of sin should trigger the same type of reaction. The recognition of what is missing helps us orient ourselves towards what must be found. The idea of "missing" creates the need for finding a solution and supplying what is lacking.

In the case of the modern church, we typically talk about what is spiritually missing and needs to be found in terms of righteousness (see Chapter 4). For now, we'll define it as right standing with God. Sin is the idea that we recognize a wrong standing, moral or otherwise, which should have been a right standing. We shouldn't have missed the mark. We shouldn't fall short of the standard. Yet marks and standards are seemingly missed more often than not, requiring our attention.

Potholes, Math Tests and Standard Missers
What do we do with the pothole? Fill it. Cover it. Provide that which was lacking. What do we do with an incorrect math problem? Solve it. Replace that which was missing by supplying the correct answer.

Whether to miss, stray, not reach, lack, or fail to meet the standard, there are so many ways to describe the concept of sin using words people understand. Let us be well versed in them so we might have the joy of being part of illuminating the biblical text for others, shedding light on words that have seemed shrouded in the shadows of mystery.

In every possible way, all human beings miss the standards God has fully intended for us to meet. In fact, it is now in our very nature to miss the standards. We are Standard Missers. They say golf is "a game of misses," but now that sin has infected the human race, each one of our experiences becomes "a life of misses."

Physically, emotionally, morally, ethically, spiritually, creatively, vocationally, managerially, practically—we all fall short of His all-encompassing standards and thus, our plight is utterly hopeless outside of a dramatic intrusion on our behalf. This is why the sacrifice of Christ on the cross is so important to all of life, both in eternity and today. The cross is the dramatic rescue on our behalf. It is the avenue for reconciliation with God and with ourselves both individually and collectively.

Without the cross of Christ, we are fractured, frustrated, and dismayed. Through faith in Jesus Christ, the One who died for sin and rose from the dead, we enjoy the forgiveness of sin (of missing the mark, of being lost, broken, etc.) and the enabling presence of the Holy Spirit. This enabling presence allows us to participate with the Lord and His ongoing plans for our full reconciliation to Him and others. Such an endeavor is indeed a grand and glorious thought as so beautifully penned by Horatio Spafford in *It Is Well With My Soul*:

> My sin, oh, the bliss of this glorious thought!
> My sin, not in part but the whole,
> Is nailed to the cross, and I bear it no more,
> Praise the Lord, praise the Lord, O my soul!

For further study:

Genesis 4:7	Isaiah 59:2	1 Corinthians 15:56
Genesis 31:39	John 1:29	James 1:15
Ex. 32:30-35	Romans 5:12-20	
Proverbs 19:2	Romans 6:1-23	

CHAPTER 3

FAITH
Aman | Pisteuō

By faith we see the hand of God
In the light of creation's grand design
In the lives of those who prove His faithfulness
Who walk by faith and not by sight.
By Faith
Keith Getty, Kristyn Getty, Stuart Townsend

When the world's coming at you like a hungry alligator
You got to have faith
When you've got to pay them now or they'll take it from
you later
You got to have faith
When you feel like the future's hiding on a distant cloud
You got to have faith
And you feel like shouting at the good Lord out loud
You got to have faith.
Faith
Air Supply

Abraham believed in the Lord;
and it was reckoned to him as righteousness.
Genesis 15:6

OUR NEXT WORD IS FAITH, intentionally placed directly after our study of sin. Faith begins to tell us the story of the remedy for sin. The first five words we are studying outline a conceptual understanding of the gospel. **Helper** told us of the perfection soon ruined by **sin,** which can be remedied by **faith**, which renders the believer **righteous** before God, which we refer to as "being **saved**" or **salvation**. The later set of our key words will tell us more about the God who orchestrated this marvelous plan of salvation, bringing us back to right standing with him and the hope of a sinless future.

The Hebrew root verb for the idea of "to believe" or "have faith" is *aman*. This is the term from which we get the word that draws our prayers to a close—amen. At its core, *aman* means "it is so," and amen means "let it be so." Therefore, when we pray, we are asking God that all we just said may become reality or become "so." The verb *pisteuō* (*pístis* - noun) is the Greek form and conveys the same idea as the Hebrew *aman* word family. To illustrate, Paul uses *pisteuō* in Romans 4:3 when he directly quotes Genesis 15:6—"Abraham *believed* (*aman*) God and it was credited to him as righteousness."

As our word studies are "key" biblical terms, they will often have similar direct conceptual correlations between Hebrew and Greek (and therefore the Old and New Testaments). So in this case, when it comes to faith, *aman* and *pisteuō* mean the same thing. The concept of faith remains consistent throughout the text.

Remember the trashcan I had in my classroom I told you about in the last chapter? The one in which I told my students to "throw away" their Christian lingo? It's time to do it again. So, for a moment, let's toss the word "faith," along with its synonyms "belief" and "trust," and see if we can still describe what they mean.

The rubber sure meets the road quickly when we do this, doesn't it? Faith is a word we use all the time, but can we define it without using the normal descriptors of believe or trust? Let's consider some word pictures, from both modern life as well as the biblical text, that will bring clarity and help us better understand this key word.

Strength is the Key

Let's begin with the concept that faith is the recognition of **strength** in someone or something, and then relying upon the strength of that someone or something. We are all looking for something on which to rely, right? And we are only willing to rely upon that which we have decided is strong, that which we believe will not fail us.

When you sit in a chair, you probably don't demand to first speak to the builder of the chair, or pick the chair up, turning it every which way to assess it. Instead, you see the chair is similar to one that has held you before, like all the chairs that have never failed you in the past, and you take a seat. It is likely not even a conscious thought because sitting in chairs is such a normal part of life. You see a chair and sit in it.

If, however, you see a chair off in the corner, the seat a bit tattered and a leg twisted or broken, it is likely neither you nor anyone else will choose the chair, bring it to the table or into the circle, and sit in it. Why? Because it is clear the chair has been deemed not strong enough to rely upon, and therefore set aside, away from the reliable seats.

Faith is a reaction to the perception of strength and typically results in reliance upon that which is deemed strong. We put our faith in something we have determined to be dependable—**able** to be depended upon. It is reliable—**able** to be relied upon. We have assessed the strength and determined it to be sufficient.

We know, of course, sometimes we assess something as reliable or dependable and then discover that it is not. Have you ever put your foot on the brake and found the car refusing to slow down? That which you had assessed as reliable and dependable (for good reason, as the brakes of your car have worked far more often than not just as you believed they would) proved not to be. So, our assessments are not always perfect, which is why faith in God is the only faith that always proves sufficient— because the object of the faith is supremely strong and perfect.

As we begin to form a word picture for the idea of faith, consider these words as essential to its concept:
- Strong/Able
- Steady/Steadfast
- Sure
- Firm
- Secure
- Support
- Dependable
- Reliable
- Entrust

The Faith of Abraham

Let us begin our time investigating biblical uses of faith in Genesis 15:6, where "Abraham *believed* in the Lord; and it was reckoned to him as righteousness." (You might recall this statement is also quoted in Romans 4.) Take note of the fact that the result of belief (faith) is righteousness, the word we will study in our next chapter. That's a key transaction throughout Scripture—**faith in the Lord results in the believer having a "right standing" (or righteousness) in the eyes of the Lord.**

Examples of Faith

Now we'll consider in Scripture some examples of faith that are not theological, i.e., God is not the one talking and/or the primary subject. Rather, these are examples that simply refer to the various ways people communicated in normal day-to-day dialogue, using common words of their time.

Exodus 17 records an unusual military encounter between Israel and the Amalekites. Moses instructed Joshua to round up soldiers and then (with Aaron and Hur and his staff) he took his place on the top of a hill overlooking the battlefield. It was soon discovered Moses' hands were the key to Israel's fate in the battle. Verse 11 informs us, "When Moses held his hands up, Israel prevailed, and when he let his hands down, Amalek prevailed." All that was needed for Israel to win was for Moses to keep his hands and staff in the air!

Exodus 17:12 states, "But Moses' hands were heavy. Then they took a stone and put it under him, and he sat on it; and Aaron and Hur supported his hands, one on one side and one on the other. Thus his hands were *steady* and sure." The strength of Aaron and Hur was used to make Moses' hands *steady,* to make his hands "*aman,*" if you will. Aaron and Hur's support of Moses may have been for a spiritual purpose, but the act of using their arms to *steady* Moses' arms was physical and practical, not inherently theological.

In Exodus 18:21, we read, "You shall select out of all the people able men...men of *truth*...and you shall place these over them, as leaders." *Truth* is the noun form of *aman.* The same word translated elsewhere as faith and steady is translated here as truth. The men are considered trustworthy because they are fixed on reliable and dependable information. They are steady, they are sure.

Master Workman, Artists, Doorposts and Nurses

Proverbs 8:30 reads, "Then I was beside Him, as a *master workman*; and I was daily His delight, rejoicing always before Him." Here we see the noun form of *aman* translated as "master workman," which will require a bit more conceptual thinking on our part.

The Book of Proverbs is primarily intended to endow the reader with wisdom or skill, to teach him or her how to do something and do it well. Skill is the wonderful combination of not only knowing what to do but how to do it. Look around you at all the things that required skill to create—furniture, a lamp, food, clothes, a clock. These items came about because someone was taught the skill required to know how to make them and implemented that skill effectively.

The narrator in Proverbs 8 is wisdom (a feminine noun in Hebrew), and in verse 30 she says she was with God when He created the world. "Let me tell you," she says to us, "He knew what He was doing." He is reliable, He is sure, He is able to be depended upon, and He is the essence of faith. He is a master workman, the master craftsman of the universe.

Another example similar to the master workman is found in Jeremiah 52:15, which says, "Then Nebuzaradan the captain of the guard carried away into exile some of the poorest of the people, the rest of the people who were left in the city, the deserters who had deserted to the king of Babylon and the rest of the *artisans*." The noun form of *aman* here is translated as "artisans." Why? Because the skilled craftspeople, the men and women who know how to build and mold and design and create things with their hands, they are well established in their trade. They are sure, reliable, and dependable as artists and fashioners of goods. They can be counted upon.

Imagine you attend a garage sale and spot a painting you'd like to buy. You approach the seller and ask the price. She says, "That painting is three dollars." You want to barter a little, so you say, "How about one dollar?" She offers to sell it to you for two dollars and you take the deal. After hanging the painting at home, you notice a smudge in the bottom-right corner and wipe it away. Lo and behold, the smudge was covering up the artist's name, and you've now revealed it. "Claude Monet."

Suddenly, your opinion of the painting has shifted entirely. Rather than seeing it as a decent find at a garage sale, it's now a work of art from a master painter! You ascribe weight, value, and prestige to it because you (and many others!) are sure the artist knew what he was doing—his art is dependable. This is why wisdom is like a master workman, why *aman* is used to speak of artists.

I once had the opportunity to stand on the tee box at the 18th hole of the Augusta National Golf Club where the annual Masters tournament is played. I watched professional golfers hit their drives down the beautiful fairway. Spectators, myself included, surrounded each golfer on every side waiting for them to send that hard, little, white sphere into the air at 180 miles per hour.

Think about it. The spectators, especially those standing a few feet off to the sides but **in front of the tee box**, were (potentially) in extreme danger. The ball is about to be flying through the air and would cause detrimental harm to anyone in its path. So, why did we stand so close to the golfers? Because we knew they were so skilled, so strong in their craft that we could rely upon them to hit tee shots straight down the fairway and not towards us!

See how the concepts are weaving together? Truth, skill, master workmen, artisans, reliability, trust, dependability. All of these ideas unite to form the biblical concept of faith.

Let's add a few more threads to the tapestry of our concept of faith (*aman*). In 2 Kings 18:16 we read, "At that time Hezekiah cut off the gold from the doors of the temple of the LORD, and from the *doorposts* which Hezekiah king of Judah had overlaid, and gave it to the king of Assyria." Hezekiah is so broke from being extorted by the Assyrian king that he is taking the gold overlay off the doors of the temple to make his payment. The word "doorposts"—which could easily be translated "supports"—is from the *aman* word family. The doorposts (or supports) are the strong things, the reliable things, the things that will not suddenly fall.

Ruth 4:16 states, "Then Naomi took the child and laid him in her lap, and became his *nurse*." Yes, the Hebrew noun form of *aman* is translated *nurse* here! Why? A nurse is a reliable one, a supporter—dependable and resolved. Here, Naomi here assumes the role of caring for a child, of being the counted-upon one. We might use the word "professional" to describe this kind of person.

The Faith of a Roman Soldier

The way Jesus speaks of faith in the Gospels reveals a great deal about Who He is and what He thinks about faith. When it comes to matters of faith, Jesus is no respecter of persons. If you've got faith, then Jesus makes note of it. It doesn't matter who you are—your background, your gender, your social status, your ethnicity, your job—your faith is of utmost importance to Christ. And here's the kicker—Jesus likes to evaluate or "grade" faith!

Take Matthew 8, for example. Jesus has just finished His famous Sermon on the Mount (Matthew 5-7). In the final two verses of Matthew 7, we see a quick summary of the sermon, "When Jesus had finished these words, the crowds were amazed at His teaching for He was teaching them as one having authority, and not as their scribes." Jesus taught with "authority."

As Chapter 8 begins, there is no break in the action as Jesus comes down from the mountain where He had just delivered the sermon, encounters a Jewish leper, and then makes His way to Capernaum, His Galilean headquarters. There, a Roman centurion approaches Jesus and implores Him to heal his servant who is "lying paralyzed at home, fearfully tormented."[1]

This Roman centurion is a fellow worth getting to know. He is a Gentile and presumed enemy of the Jews, occupying the Roman province known then as "Judaea" (or perhaps "Palestina" or "Philistia"). He is a professional soldier, having risen from the ranks to a seasoned officer. The Roman Army then was comprised of approximately 25 legions; each legion had about 5,000 men who were further divided into 60 "centuries." A century totaled 80 men, similar to the American concept of a "company." A centurion was in charge of one of these groups of 80 soldiers. He is a crucial member of the Roman army, having traveled the world for Rome's glory.

The centurion was probably assigned to the Roman garrison at Capernaum, located on the northern shore of

---

[1] Regarding the term "servant" in 8:6, Matthew uses the Greek term *pais*, sometimes translated "child" or "young person." In the parallel account of Luke 7:10, the term "slave" (*doulos*) is used to describe the person. I'm going to assume that the person is the young servant of the centurion. The key is to note the great care the centurion expressed toward the infirmed person.

the Sea of Galilee. He is responsible for putting down civil unrest and keeping open the two north-south routes that extend through the land. Israel is the size of the state of Vermont and has long been important for its geography, and serves as a key land bridge, linking Asia and Europe to Africa. The centurion is a man's man, skilled in the art and savagery of war. He has seen many men die, often at the tip of his sword. He is tough, battle-hardened, and lives in a world of rank, order, discipline, and authority.

Jesus immediately offers to go with the centurion to his home and heal the servant but the centurion says in Matthew 8:8-9, "...Lord, I am not worthy for You to come under my roof, **but just say the word**, and my servant will be healed. For I also am a man under **authority**, with soldiers under me; and I say to this one, 'Go!' and he goes, and to another, 'Come!' and he comes, and to my slave, 'Do this!' and he does it.'"

Did you see it? In essence, the centurion rejects Jesus' offer to go to his home and heal the servant in person. He tells Jesus he is not worthy of His presence in his house where the servant lies in anguish. The centurion concludes that it is not necessary for Jesus to personally go to the servant to heal him. This is the moment that reveals the exceptional quality of the centurion's faith.

The centurion's faith is in the authority of Jesus. Remember the author's summary of Jesus' sermon at the end of Chapter 7? Matthew wrote that Jesus was teaching with "authority." And so here, just a few verses later in Matthew 8:9, the centurion illustrates the point in recognizing the great **authority** of Jesus as well. After all, the soldier also lives in a world of authority. Military life is about giving orders, receiving orders. Quick, efficient, effective, military dispatch. All Jesus has to do is "say the word" and the servant would be healed.

Jesus marvels at the centurion's words and responds in 8:10, "Truly I say to you, I have not found such **great** *faith* (*pístis*) with anyone in Israel." He then goes on to heal the servant "...as you have *believed* (*pisteuō*)..." in 8:13. It is remarkable this occurred at all, and all the more that it is recorded in Matthew, the most Jewish of the four gospels. For the Jews to learn not only that a Roman soldier (a Gentile!) had faith in Jesus, but also a faith **greater than** anyone in Israel, was absolutely scandalous. And if this wasn't enough, Jesus does it again.

The Faith of a Canaanite Woman

The grisly, senseless death of John the Baptist (Matthew 14) was a huge blow to the ministry of Jesus and the disciples. Things had been going pretty well overall. Opposition was stiffening, certainly, but John's death seemed to set a much harsher tone leading to the crucifixion. Jesus' reactions to the tragedy are noteworthy. Twice He withdraws to lonely places (14:13, 23). He feeds 5,000 (14:21). He walks on water (14:26). And for the first and only time during the earthly ministry of Jesus, He and the disciples leave Judea. He leads them to the district of Tyre and Sidon (15:21), modern-day Lebanon. This is land long-held by enemies of the Jews. This is Canaanite country, the same Canaan cursed by Noah in Genesis 9. Sidon is the firstborn son of Canaan (Genesis 10:15) and namesake for the rich Mediterranean port town about 25 miles south of Beirut. Tyre, 20 miles south of Sidon, is another coastal city, replete with merchants and commerce. Tyre was the home of Jezebel (1 Kings 16:31-32) and is the second-most despised city in the Bible, only behind Babylon. During the first century, these towns were known for trade, shipping, luxury, recreation, and pagan idolatry. Weary sailors, home from long voyages at sea, found refreshment of all kinds in these towns' brothels, pagan temples, and local establishments.

So, with this ominous backdrop, Matthew 15:22 records, "And a Canaanite woman from that region came out and began to cry out, saying, 'Have mercy on me, Lord, Son of David; my daughter is cruelly demon-possessed.'" Let's take a moment for some observations. She's described as a "Canaanite," the sole occurrence of this term in the New Testament. She asks for mercy. She calls Jesus "Lord" and "Son of David." She has a daughter. The daughter has a demon. Now if you're a disciple of Jesus, fresh off the cruel killing of John, in enemy territory, in a region full of idol worship and religious debauchery, perhaps this lady fulfills all your fears, all your long-held prejudices. After all, she's a Canaanite. What good could she ever produce? And her daughter? Demon possessed, of course. Pagan idolatry attracts such things, you know. But, wait a minute. Yes, she is a Canaanite. Yes, she does have a daughter who is possessed by a demon. But, what else is there about her? She calls Jesus "Lord," but that could be just a title of respect, like "sir." But she also calls Him, "Son of David." No way to spin this expression. It is a well-known term for the long-promised "greater" son of David, the prophesied King, and the long-awaited Messiah. She recognizes Jesus as the Messiah.

Ever the Master Teacher, Jesus does not immediately respond to her initial cry. Paradoxically, the disciples implore Him to send her away because she is "shouting at us." (15:23). The disciples are not presented in the best light here, beautifully setting the stage for the faith of the Canaanite woman to be revealed. Perhaps we can understand the attitude of the disciples. Exhausted from the trip, despondent over the death of John the Baptist, they've had enough of "other" people for a while. Let's see how this turns out.

The story continues in Matthew 15:24-28, "But He answered and said, 'I was sent only to the lost sheep of the house of Israel.' But she came and began to bow down before Him, saying, 'Lord, help me!' And He answered and said, 'It is not good to take the children's bread and throw it to the dogs.' But she said, 'Yes, Lord; but even the dogs feed on the crumbs which fall from their masters' table.' Then Jesus said to her, 'O woman, your *faith* (*pístis*) is **great**; it shall be done for you as you wish.' And her daughter was healed at once."

Yet again, Jesus refers to a Gentile as having "great faith." What is the key to her faith? What does she understand about Jesus that separates her from the pack? Is it the fact that she identifies Jesus as the "Son of David"? Probably not, although given her background and physical separation from Jesus' ministry in Judea, it's quite remarkable she refers to Him as such. I think it's the "crumb" reference that puts her in the elite faith level.

Despite the faithless outcries of the disciples, she has persisted in her conversation with Jesus. She basically ignores His statement about His being sent only to Israel. She personalizes the problem ("Lord, help me!") and awaits His response. Jesus changes the scene to one of a family sitting down to dinner. Let's assume the father and mother are present. We know the children are present. There's food, including bread, which has been prepared and brought to the table. There are a couple of dogs under the table or perhaps roaming about outside. Jesus says to her in 15:26, "…it is not good to take the children's bread and throw it to the dogs." Now here's a scene that even a Canaanite woman whose daughter has a demon can handle! Before she responds, let's listen in on her thoughts: "You want to talk about dinnertime, and kids, and bread portions for kids, and dogs? OK, I got this. I agree it's not good to take the bread that was intended for the kids and throw it to the dogs. But what about the crumbs...who gets them?"

Her actual response, recorded in Matthew 15:27, is now seen, "But she said, 'yes, Lord; but even the dogs feed on the crumbs which fall from their masters' table.'" She knows Jesus is not calling her a "dog." In fact, they both use a common word for "little dogs," in keeping with the dinnertime scene. She knows that bread prepared for children is not to be given to dogs instead. But she also knows crumbs sometimes fall to the floor and the dogs enjoy a morsel. That's all she is asking for. Not a seat at the table. Not the whole loaf of bread. Not even a child's portion of bread. Just a crumb, but not any crumb. She is asking for a crumb that might fall from the Master's table, from bread baked by the Son of David! She recognizes the great **sufficiency** of Jesus. He's enough, even His crumbs.

The Great Faithers

The Roman centurion and the Canaanite woman are the **only two individuals** whom Jesus commended as demonstrating "great faith" in Scripture. Never once did He evaluate the faith of the disciples as "great." Instead, they often heard these stinging words, "You of little faith" (Matthew 6:30, 8:26, 14:31, 16:8, 17:20, and Luke 12:28). These two alone carry the lofty distinction as "The Great Faithers." Great Faithers see Jesus in a different way, a more complete and realistic way, and adjust and respond to Him accordingly. These two Great Faithers provide us specific ways to demonstrate faith in the

Lord—full respect of the authority and sufficiency of Jesus Christ.

The centurion taught us the **authority** of Jesus is like that of Five-Star Generals. Their authority is unchallenged. Their authority is powerful. Their authority is effective. This is why the centurion found it unnecessary for Jesus to visit his suffering servant. Distance is no obstacle for such authority. Physical presence is not necessary for such authority. All you need is a word from one with such authority. The Canaanite woman taught us of the **sufficiency** of Jesus. Of course, Jesus does not extend mere crumbs to us, but even if He did, we should find them sufficient. It would be enough. The bread prepared by the Master Himself is ample for our sustenance. His authority. His sufficiency. The keys to great faith.

Key New Testament Verses

Hebrews 11:1 states, "Now *faith* (*pístis*) is the assurance of things hoped for, the conviction of things not seen." The word for assurance here is *hypostasis*, which means that which stands under or, similarly to 2 Kings 18, supports. "Conviction" is a translation of *elegchos*, which means proof. So, faith is the recognition of worthy support, that which strongly stands under us, the proof we bank on.

Romans 4:1-5 tells us, "Now to the one who works, his wage is not credited as a favor, but as what is due. But to the one who does not work, but *believes* in Him who justifies the ungodly, his faith is credited as righteousness." Faith in the object, God, produces a right standing with Him, which we will look into even more in our next chapter on righteousness.

Wrapping Up

When I was a builder, I worked with a man named Ricky from Alabama. He had a habit of nailing something in, walking away confidently, and saying through his thick southern accent, "That ain't goin' nowhere!" He was absolutely sure, because he trusted the strength of his work, the sureness of the lumber, the solidity of the nails. He had faith in the strong things.

Let's take a look at some other builders and offer a final word picture for your consideration. There is a famous photograph taken in 1932 of 11 men sitting on a beam during the construction of a skyscraper originally called the RCA Building, then the GE Building, and now the Comcast Building. Its address is 30 Rockefeller Plaza (or "30 Rock") in New York City. The men are steelworkers, casually eating lunch while sitting on a beam some 840-feet up in the air. There are no nets, no ropes. OSHA will not be founded until some 40 years later!

The picture causes sheer panic in me, but the men in the picture are as calm as can be. How can they be so calm? Because they have been there all along, building the structure from the ground up. They personally handled each and every steel beam. They made sure the beams were level, plumb, and true. They made sure the rivets were driven solidly, the frame secured. They were sure of its reliability and thus did not need to fear.

Similarly, in fact all the more, we can be so very sure of the strength and dependability of our great God; and because He is so reliable, we can entrust ourselves to Him more and more. Indeed, He is strong. He is sure. He is so. He ain't goin' nowhere!

For further study:

Proverbs 19:2	Psalm 78:37	Psalm 89:37
1 Samuel 2:35	Deut. 27:15-26	Habakkuk 2:4
Romans 1:17	Hebrews 11	

CHAPTER 4

RIGHTEOUS
Tsaddiq | Dikaiosynē

My hope is built on nothing less
than Jesus' blood and righteousness.
I dare not trust the sweetest frame,
but wholly lean on Jesus' name.
My Hope is Built on Nothing Less
Edward Mote

May you grow up to be righteous
May you grow up to be true
May you always know the truth
And see the lights surrounding you
May you always be courageous
Stand upright and be strong
And may you stay
Forever young.
Forever Young
Bob Dylan

Noah was a righteous man, blameless in his time;
Noah walked with God.
Then the LORD said to Noah,
"Enter the ark, you and all your household;
for you alone I have seen
to be righteous before Me in this time."
Genesis 6:9; 7:1

THE GOSPEL (which, remember, simply means "good news") addresses the giant problem of sin. Faith in Jesus, who died for our sins and rose from the dead, makes us righteous. We are now going to take a look at the concept of righteousness, of being made right with God.

The common Old Testament root word for righteous is *tsaddiq* (from *tsedeq*), as transliterated in the latter half of the word Melchi*zidek*, and which conveys the concept of righteousness or meeting (or satisfying) a standard. The most common New Testament expression of the same concept is the noun *dikaiosynē*, which carries the idea of meeting a standard, or righteousness.

"Righteous" is a concept almost the exact opposite of the biblical idea of sin. Sin is failing to meet or conform to the standard; righteousness is the seal, the stamp, the verdict that declares we have met the standard. The words for righteous in the Old and New Testaments can also be translated "just" or "justified."

The first time this term appears in Scripture is in Genesis 6, when God says, "Noah was a righteous man, blameless in his time; Noah walked with God," and again in Genesis 7, "Then the LORD said to Noah, 'Enter the ark, you and all your household; for you alone I have seen to be righteous before Me in this time.'" These usages of righteous certainly point to a spiritual reality relevant to salvation, but there are other usages of the word that are not theological.

In the book of Deuteronomy (which means "second law"), God gives the Mosaic Law to a new generation of Israelites, explaining to them how to relate to Him and one another. These laws included everything from how to offer sacrifices for sin to how to care for wounds on their arms. They also included instructions on proper conduct in the marketplace—a cornerstone of human interactions.

The Scales Don't Lie

Life is full of universal scales that are not ours to tip. Gallons, kilograms, miles, feet, yards, meters, pounds…these are all units of measurement to which things must conform. A foot is always 12 inches. A mile always meets the standard of 5,280 feet. Five pounds of potatoes weighs five pounds. A gallon of milk is always, well, a gallon of milk! Why? Because the common standards have been set and they must be met. Without common standards, humanity would be at a loss as to how to function in the world, for what is and is not true, for how to buy food or travel or treat medical problems. We need universal scales and common standards, and we need them to be met.

When it comes to sin and righteousness, we can learn what God wants us to know from a fourth-grade math quiz. The teacher grades the problems and marks those that are correct as "right" and the incorrect ones as "wrong"—or "sins," if we recall the biblical definition. As we discussed earlier, we tend to shrivel up at the idea of the word sin because we so often ascribe moral failure to it. But, as we have already seen in the second chapter— sin often refers to non-moral failures to meet a standard.

Similarly, righteousness often refers to the meeting of a moral standard and other times it describes the meeting of a non-moral standard. Righteous in Scripture can, and often does, simply imply remaining consistent with universal human codes and scales. The key is to determine which type of standard (moral or non-moral) best fits each biblical context when a form of the term righteous is used.

Grocery Store Education

Deuteronomy 25:13-15 says, "You shall not have in your bag differing weights, a large and a small. You shall not have in your house differing measures, a large and a small. You shall have a full and *just* weight; you shall have a full and *just* measure." Here, *tsaddiq* is translated "just."

God tells the Israelites they cannot use one weight that benefits them when they are the seller and another that benefits them when they are the buyer. Rather, they are to have one "full and *just* measure," a weight that is accurate and ensures fairness for those on both sides of the transaction. The weight should be normal, meeting and conforming to a standard.

There's an iconic image from The Saturday Evening Post in which a buyer and seller are looking at the number on the scale holding a plump chicken ready for purchase. If you look carefully at their faces, you may think they're just especially committed to precision, but their fingers tell the real story (which is quite the opposite). The buyer's hand is underneath the scale, trying to hold it up and therefore reduce the weight reflected on the scale, while the seller is pushing down on the scale to cause greater weight to be reflected. The image is comical of course, but it is also indicative of the exact human desire God is addressing in Deuteronomy 25. As humans, we are forever facing and often indulging the temptation to tip the scales in our favor, rather than conforming to the standard established before us and which exists outside of us.

God Loves Righteousness

Psalm 11:7a states, "For the LORD is *righteous*; He loves *righteousness*." God Himself is the standard for righteousness. And not only that, He loves being the standard for righteousness! This is a fundamental fact about the character and essence of God, and it should impact our recognition of the standards He sets, as well the arrangement of our lives to meet them.

Consider the relationship of Psalm 11:7 with Matthew 6:33, which reads, "But seek first His kingdom and His *righteousness*, and all these things will be added to you." We are not merely to observe the standards God has set, recognizing them and then working them in when it seems convenient. **Rather, we are to orient our lives to meet God's standards**. The calling on the life of the Christian is to seek that which God has established, that which He considers to be righteous, first, above all else.

Psalm 145:17a states, "The Lord is *righteous* in all His ways…" Read it again, slowly, and consider the fundamental truths of the verse. What is it telling us? It is telling us God is always righteous and He sets the standard for righteousness—He cannot walk away from righteousness or step outside of it even for a moment, even for one action. Righteousness is the essence of His character and the unstoppable, consistent outflow of His actions. In His very being and every action, God can be nothing but righteous, for it is His very substance.

The Righteous One

In Isaiah 53:11 we read, "As a result of the anguish of His soul, He will see it and be satisfied; by His knowledge the *Righteous* One, My Servant, will *justify* the many, as He will bear their iniquities." Scripture is telling us here the Righteous One—the One who possesses and attains the standard—will also be the One who makes others righteous. Interestingly, Isaiah uses different forms of *tsaddiq* to construct an adjective (the Righteous One), as well as a verb (will justify the many), in the same verse.

This prophecy tells us of the One who will bear the iniquities of others and make them right, which is the essence of salvation—one being transferred from wrong standing with God to right standing.

The word "righteous" is a fundamental building block of a key verse in all of Scripture—Genesis 15:6. It reads "then he [Abram] believed in the Lord; and He reckoned it to him as *righteousness.*" Here, we see the transaction between faith and God's provision for our sin explicitly explained. When one believes in the Lord, it is counted as righteousness for him or her. Faith in the Lord is a transaction in which the believer is made right before God.

The Bleeding Pharisees

In Matthew 5:20, Jesus is preaching the Sermon on the Mount and states, "For I say to you, that unless your *righteousness* (*dikaiosynē*) surpasses that of the scribes and Pharisees, you shall not enter the kingdom of heaven." The idea of righteousness needing to surpass something again conjures up the image of a standard—not only must the righteousness noted reach a certain level, but surpass it, stretching beyond what is already a lofty goal.

An interesting example of this is a group known as The Bleeding Pharisees. This particular sect of Pharisees had arranged their lives around the seventh commandment as seen in Exodus 20:14, "You shall not commit adultery." They considered this commandment as their entire standard of righteousness. So, they obsessively thought about what could lead to committing adultery and adopted the idea that if they never even looked upon a woman, then the odds of actually committing adultery with a woman went down dramatically. Let's see how that worked out for them!

Of course, the idea of making it through a day without seeing a member of half of the population is a bit of a challenge. In their fervor, these men determined to walk around in public with their heads down, virtually rendering themselves incapable of seeing a woman (or at least any more than her feet). So, they became known as "The Bleeding Pharisees." As they walked around with their heads down, they endured frequent collisions with low-hanging obstacles, causing cuts and scrapes and bruises all over the tops of their heads. They wore those wounds and scars like badges of honor in their zealous striving for righteousness.

As ridiculous as their behavior may seem to us, I would guess there is a part of your heart that resonates with it as part of mine does. We know on one level to follow God doesn't require such extreme measures. However, we can also feel the same pull in us—the temptation to pick one of God's requirements and obsess about it so greatly that we convince ourselves that righteousness can be ours if we are meeting this one particular standard.

But look at Matthew 5:20 again, "...unless your *righteousness* **surpasses** that of the scribes and Pharisees, you shall not enter the kingdom of heaven." I don't know about you, but I haven't given myself any head wounds bumping into shelves or hanging plants to avoid adultery! Jesus, of course, is explaining to the audience at the Sermon on the Mount, as well as to us, that righteousness cannot be achieved by man's independent pursuit of God's standard. It can only be achieved by God making a way.

Righteousness From God

Paul illustrates this fact in Philippians 3:9. He writes, "And may be found in Him, not having a *righteousness* of my own derived from the Law, but that which is through faith in Christ, the *righteousness* which comes from God on the basis of faith…" Paul is clear as can be—no human is capable of satisfying the standard of God's Law on his or her own. There is no hope for man to check every box, obey every rule, be ruled by right thinking, feeling, saying, doing. We need someone else to be the righteous one on our behalf, which is of course what makes the gospel so beautiful. Jesus was, and is the Righteous One who lived a perfect life, died a sacrificial death, and rose in victory that we, hidden in Him, may be seen righteous before the Father who is righteous in His essence and every action.

Let's consider two more examples together as these speak to the Christian's status as a righteous one before God. In Daniel 12:3 we read, "Those who have insight will shine brightly like the brightness of the expanse of heaven, and those who lead the many to *righteousness*, like the stars forever and ever." God's law illuminates us, shedding light on us internally and flowing from us externally, guiding others to see Who He is and what He has done for humanity.

This verse is so very full of hope for believers. We are the brightly shining ones because God has made a way. We can lead others to righteousness because God has made a way. We will dwell eternally in peace with God, like the stars, because God has made a way.

In 1 John 1:9 we are reminded that righteousness is essentially the opposite of sin. "If we confess our sins," we read, "He is faithful and righteous to forgive us our sins and to cleanse us from all un*righteousness*." The parallel language is quite strong—sin is confessed and forgiven, unrighteousness is cleansed. Sin and unrighteousness are the same idea—they are that which does not meet the standard and thus needs to be made right for a person to enjoy a right relationship with God.

Standard Meeters

It is essential to our understanding of Scripture and the plan of salvation that we understand the biblical concept of righteousness. God is righteous and He loves righteousness—He is the standard and loves to set the standard and see it met. He is the scale and loves to see it balanced. Scripture tells us the story of this perfect God setting the perfect standard, and, as we remember from our study of sin, the standard being woefully missed just three chapters into the story of the Bible.

Yet all along, in His ferocious love for righteousness and humanity, God has offered a plan for righteousness to those who reflect His image on this earth. Ultimately, in Christ, the standard was fully met, and we were transferred from Standard Missers (sinners) to Standard Meeters (righteous ones).

As those who believe the Lord Jesus Christ died for our sins and rose from the dead, we are hidden in Him, granted right standing before God. Like Abraham, we believe God and it is credited to us as righteousness. We acknowledge we are inadequate to meet the standard God is and has set. So, as we turn in faith to Jesus, we get "saved," a term we will study in our next chapter, casting ourselves onto the Righteous One who was fully God and fully man on our behalf. Thus, we now have the capacity to conform to the standard by way of our union with Christ. We have been made right with God, so let's live accordingly.

For further study:

Genesis 14:17	Isaiah 5:22-23	Romans 6
Genesis 18:23	Jeremiah 33:16	2 Corinthians 5:21
Job 13:18	Romans 3:10-14	
Job 32:2	Romans 4	

CHAPTER 5

SAVE
Yasha | Sōzō

Amazing grace! how sweet the sound,
That saved a wretch; like me!
I once was lost, but now am found,
Was blind, but now I see.
Amazing Grace
John Newton

Shadows and the stars
We will not return
Humanity won't save us
At the speed of light
Shadows and the stars
We will not return
Humanity won't save us
We slip into the night
Forever young.
Speed of Light
Iron Maiden

Help, Lord, for the godly man ceases to be,
for the faithful disappear from among the sons of men.
"Because of the devastation of the afflicted,
now I will arise," says the Lord;
"I will set him in the safety for which he longs."
Psalm 12:1, 5

THUS FAR, WE HAVE JOURNEYED THROUGH OUR FIRST FOUR key biblical words—**helper**, which carries with it the idea of perfect completion/ harmony present before the fall; **sin**, that which is lacking or fails to meet the standard; **faith**, the recognition of the strength of something/someone and thus reliable; and **righteousness**, achieving or conforming to the standard.

When we understand these words theologically and wrap them up altogether, we often refer to that package, if you will, as **salvation**, or "getting **saved**." And so, it follows that our next word is "save", a word which, just like each word we've studied before it, is used throughout Scripture in both theological and non-theological ways.

In the Old Testament, the primary Hebrew word that we translate save is *yasha* (or *yasha'*), from which the names Joshua, Jeshua, Jehoshaphat, and Jesus are derived. In the New Testament, the Greek root term is *sōzō*. It's very important to remember both words can convey the idea of either physical or spiritual salvation. The root ideas or concepts of these words include:

- Safe/safety
- To deliver
- To rescue
- To transfer
- Save/salvation
- Savior

The Key Question

The key question for understanding this word is, "What kind of salvation is this? Is this a physical deliverance, such as from a fire or from drowning, or is it some kind of spiritual salvation? From what is the person being saved?" We should not assume every time we see the word "save" in the Bible, the topic at hand is a person being saved from hell because of belief in Jesus Christ. This is simply not true to the biblical text, and all kinds of misunderstandings and improper translations of what Scripture is saying can abound if we don't take the time to investigate carefully what type of saving is taking place in each context.

Imagine you're watching a news account of a ship and its passengers in peril at sea. You see a rescue helicopter arrive in an attempt to save those in the water and close to drowning. A rope is cast down to a person who grabs onto it and is lifted to safety. The person is not being saved spiritually, of course, but physically. Yet, it is still completely appropriate to use the word "save" to describe what has happened, correct? Let us keep that in mind as we read Scripture and come across usages of the word "save." Remember to always ask yourself, "What kind of saving is the passage referring to?"

Physical Salvation

In Exodus 14:30 we read, "Thus the LORD *saved (yasha)* Israel that day from the hand of the Egyptians, and Israel saw the Egyptians dead on the seashore." While there were certainly spiritual implications for God's intervention in the lives of the Israelites during their captivity, the saving referenced here is clearly physical. God makes a way for the physical deliverance of the nation of Israel as the Red Sea engulfs their Egyptian enemies.

Psalm 12:1,5 reads, "*Help*, Lord, for the godly man ceases to be, for the faithful disappear from among the sons of men." "Because of the devastation of the afflicted…now I will arise," says the Lord; "I will set him in the *safety* for which he longs." Derivatives from the same root word (*yasha*) are rendered "help" at the beginning of verse 1 and "safety" in verse 5. God is going to provide the physical deliverance the psalmist asks Him for, offering him bodily safety and protection.

Similarly, in Matthew 8:24-25 we read, "And behold, there arose a great storm on the sea, so that the boat was being covered with the waves; but Jesus Himself was asleep. And they came and woke Him, saying, '*save* (*sōzō*) us, Lord; we are perishing!'" The disciples are not asking to go to heaven here. They are not having a moment of spiritual clarity in which they see everything around them is chaos so they need to get right with the Lord. Rather, they are simply asking they not drown in the Sea of Galilee. They perceive their lives are in danger and they want quite simply to stay alive. The words they appropriately choose to use in seeking to protect their wellbeing are "*save* us!"

These examples from Exodus, Psalms, and Matthew should reveal to readers of Scripture not only can the word for "save" be used to describe physical deliverance, but even God can be the one doing the saving and the saving is still physical. In other words, God saves in more ways than spiritually. This neither diminishes nor marginalizes His power to save spiritually in the least. Rather, it should comfort us to know our God is capable of all kinds of saving, all kinds of deliverance. And, in terms of the word usage itself, it should simply remind us to be careful and precise when we look at words in Scripture, doing our due diligence to parse out meaning where we may be prone to make assumptions.

Mark 6:56 states, "Whenever He entered villages, or cities, or countryside, they were laying the sick in the market places, and imploring Him that they might just touch the fringe of His cloak; and as many as touched it were being *cured*." *Sōzō* is translated as "cured" here, which adds a new layer of concept to our understanding of the word. The sick that touch Jesus are being delivered from illness into wellness, transferred from the danger of sickness to the safety of health.

John 11:11-12 says, "...after that He said to them, 'our friend Lazarus has fallen asleep; but I go, so that I may awaken him out of sleep.' The disciples then said to Him, 'Lord, if he has fallen asleep, he will *recover*.'" Jesus is using "fallen asleep" as a metaphor for death, claiming He will go and resurrect Lazarus from the dead. The disciples, however, think Jesus is referring to actual, normal sleep, so they say, "Lord, if he has fallen asleep, he will *recover*." Recover is *sōzō*. The disciples are saying Lazarus will wake up; he will be transferred from sleep into awareness, delivered from slumber to cognizance.

These non-theological usages will serve us well as we begin to look at usages of save or salvation in Scripture that are more likely along the lines of how we think of these words being used all the time—in a spiritual and eternal sense. Thus far, we've gathered that "save" paints a picture of someone being rescued from danger and brought to safety or transferred from a perilously ill situation to stability and health. We've seen to be saved is to be moved out of that which is or could be causing harm (or in the case of sleep, simply that which is not meant to go on forever), so that one may be brought into a better, safer place. Bear these word pictures, ideas, and concepts in mind as we turn to some of the theological uses of *yasha and sōzō* in the OT and NT.

Spiritual Salvation

In Psalm 25:5 we read, "Lead me in Your truth and teach me, for You are the God of my *salvation*; for You I wait all the day." It seems the author, David, is referring here both to his ultimate deliverance from sin through faith, and his ongoing deliverance from the wiles of sin through God's grace and David's orientation of his life around the Law of God. By asking God to lead him, David is testifying to the fact that he is fully aware only God can bring about the spiritual salvation man needs to have true righteousness, both in terms of being ultimately justified before God, and in terms of living a life that is pleasing to Him.

Acts 4:12 states, "And there is *salvation* in no one else; for there is no other name under heaven that has been given among men, by which we must be *saved*." In this verse, we see *sōzō* first as a noun (*sōtēria*, as seen in "soteriology," the study of the doctrine of salvation) and then as a verb. This verse is a good example of spiritual deliverance, perhaps more like how we typically use the word "saved" in Christian contexts. A common question in many church communities is "when did you get saved?" Or we'll begin to get to know a fellow believer a bit better by saying something like, "I'd love for you to tell me about your journey to salvation." The Acts 4:12 usage of salvation and saved is the closest we've seen of the verses we've studied so far to those usages we commonly employ within Christian circles.

Consider, though, how much more robust and meaningful the words "save" and "salvation" are in Acts 4:12 if you take a moment to ponder our word pictures from the non-theological usages. For example, you could re-read Acts 4:12 and insert brief concepts you've formed earlier in the chapter. Mine would be something like, "And there is (rescue from ultimate danger to safety and flourishing) in no one else; for there is no other name under heaven that has been given among men, by which we must be (transferred from the threat of impending death to abundant life)." By developing thicker, more colorful understandings of the key biblical word "save", we can not only read Scripture more precisely, but the way we speak and describe the experience of the Christian life both within and outside the household of faith can take on a new vibrancy.

Past, Present and Future Salvation

Titus 3:4-6 says, "But when the kindness of God our *Savior* (*sōtēria*) and His love for mankind appeared, He *saved* (*sōzō*) us, not on the basis of deeds which we have done in righteousness, but according to His mercy...through Jesus Christ our *Savior* (*sōtēria*)." This verse is referring to salvation past, which we refer to as justification (or "declared righteousness"), the result of the moment when a person believed in the Lord Jesus Christ and was "saved." Titus 3:4-6 makes clear that the moment of justification is permanent and fixed, and cannot be removed from the believer.

Philippians 2:12-13 states, however, "So then, my beloved, just as you have always obeyed...work out your *salvation* (*sōtēria*) with fear and trembling; for it is God who is at work in you, both to will and to work for His good pleasure." This use of save is referring to ongoing sanctification, which is the present salvation we experience as we are being made holy (a word we will study later). Salvation, as we saw in the case of David in Psalm 25, has some nuance to it and can be used to describe the ongoing life of the believer as he or she faithfully walks with God. Our salvation past, the moment of justification, cannot be changed or revoked, while our sanctification is a life-long process that should progress towards spiritual maturity, but may have some bumps along the road.

For the Christian, justification is in the past and sanctification is the present. And yet there is something grand that awaits us, the removal of the very presence of sin. As people who are exposed to pain and sin and despair and death every day on this earth, we can hardly imagine such a thing. Now, sin is everywhere, like the air we breathe. But as Romans 13:11 tells us, "Do this, knowing the time, that it is already the hour for you to awaken from sleep; for now *salvation* (*sōtēria*) is nearer to us than when we believed." The third phase or aspect of salvation will be enjoyed by us someday—glorification—when sin will be entirely removed from the world and us!

Salvation Wordplay

Matthew 1:21 states, "She will bear a Son; and you shall call His name Jesus, for it is He who will *save* His people from their sins." Names in Scripture are often indicative of what was in the heart of the mother during pregnancy, or a characteristic the parents hoped to see in the child. However, this wordplay formula does not work when it comes to the name of Jesus unless we use the Hebrew term for save (*yasha*) instead of the Greek *sōzō*. The verse could then be understood this way, "…and you shall call His name, for He will "*yasha*" His people from their sins." God chose to use the same word and language for "save" in Jesus' name that the Spirit inspired Moses to use when writing of the parting of the Red Sea and David when he penned the Psalms. He is *Yeshua*, the One who can "*yasha*" us from our sins!

Wrapping Up

As we draw this chapter to a close, I want to reiterate once more the importance of asking, "From what is this person/group of people being saved?" any time we come across "save" or "salvation" in Scripture. Many times in the Bible, "save" is used to describe physical deliverance. Of course, spiritual salvation is also a key theme of the Bible. Be careful to note which type of "salvation" each context presents as you interpret the text.

Some of the things from which people are "saved" in Scripture include:

- Death
- War
- Fire
- Danger
- Sin
- Hell
- Separation
- Illness
- Sleep

Let us be careful, precise readers of the text, seeking to form nuanced, vibrant understandings of these key biblical words so that we may love and live according to their truth all the more fully.

For further study:

Deut. 20:1-4	Acts 14:9	2 Cor. 5:21
1 Samuel 7:8	Acts 27:20	Ephesians 2:8-9
Psalm 51:1-2; 12	1 Cor. 1:18	Titus 2:13
Isaiah 60:16b	1 Cor. 15:1-2a	1 John 4:14
Luke 2:11	2 Cor. 2:15	

CHAPTER 6

GRACE
Chen | Cháris

Was it for crimes that I had done
He groaned upon the tree?
Amazing pity, grace unknown,
And love beyond degree!
Alas! And Did My Savior Bleed
Isaac Watts

Hey, do you want to make a difference?
Well stand in the line,
If you haven't got the time,
I can give you some of mine,
Never for the grace of god go you...And I,
We're the brightest objects in the sky,
Never for the grace of god go you...And I,
Do some good before you say goodbye.
Everybody out There
Paul McCartney

The Lord bless you, and keep you;
The Lord make His face shine on you,
and be gracious to you;
The Lord lift up His countenance on you,
and give you peace.
Numbers 6:24-26

WE HAVE MADE IT TO THE HALFWAY POINT on our journey of unlocking key biblical words. The first five words—helper, sin, faith, righteous, and save—can all be wrapped up together in such a way telling the story of humanity's need for a Savior and God's provision of one through Jesus Christ. The next six words can be seen as a set or group as well—each of them reveals characteristics that comprise this seemingly unfathomable God who would create a world, allow it to be infiltrated by sin, then provide a way for its redemption. The final word will call us to respond to such magnificence.

The focus of this chapter is the beautiful concept of grace. Grace is the key distinction of biblical Christianity. All other approaches to God require each person to merit a certain degree of approval from a supreme being to improve one's spiritual position. That approval can be earned by various acts of service, sacrifice, duty, and/or faithfulness. Christianity stands alone, boldly maintaining humankind's status before God is irreparable, except for the grace of God alone.

Grace is a game-changer. No act of service can earn God's approval. No one can cause God to look upon him or her with favor. No one can merit his or her way into His presence. Instead, we will see our God extend His lavish grace to His creatures throughout the Scriptures. A grace absolutely free, undeserved, with "no strings attached.

As expected, words for "grace" appear in both the Old and New Testaments. In the Hebrew Old Testament, the commonly used word is *chen* (or *hen*), the noun form of root verb *chanan*, and seen in the names Hannah and Anne. In the New Testament, the word is *cháris*, from which we get the word "charismatic" and the name "Charis."

The first use of *chen* in the Old Testament is found in Genesis 6:8, which reads, "But Noah found *favor* in the eyes of the Lord." In English, the idea of "favor" can carry the idea of trading courtesies back and forth. So, if I buy lunch this time, then you buy lunch next time. But Scripture's use of favor is much more akin to me buying lunch every time, with truly no expectation you ever will. So, Noah does not find a "lunch buddy" in the Lord, one where Noah will exist in a fair partnership and thus be sure to keep his end of the bargain. Rather, he finds wildly unmerited favor, a free offering from a good God who seeks no repayment. Let's keep this in mind as we continue to look through the rest of Scripture for instances of *chen* and *cháris*.

Zip, Nada, Zilch

The concept of grace will remain consistent through the two testaments and encompasses a host of nuances. The first is the notion of "nothing." This may seem a bit confusing at first since we typically think of grace as something far more than *nothing*. Let's look at a few verses together to see if we can make sense of "nothing."

Genesis 29:15 states, "Laban said to Jacob, "Because you are my relative, should you therefore serve me *for nothing*? Tell me, what shall your wages be?" "For nothing" is a translation of a form of *chen*; it is "grace." Laban is acknowledging to Jacob that his work is worth something; he should be paid a wage. Were Jacob to work for free (for nothing), that would be grace. Were Laban to give Jacob payment for doing nothing at all, that would be grace. A wage is that which is earned, grace is that which was not earned or deserved. In this case, Jacob has earned a wage and Laban is intent on paying him, rather than on Jacob working "for nothing" or "for grace."

We see the use of "for nothing" again in Job 1:9 and 2:3. It reads, "Then Satan answered the Lord, 'Does Job fear God *for nothing?*'" (1:9). And the Lord said to Satan, "Have you considered My servant Job…he still holds fast his integrity, although you incited Me against him, to ruin him *without cause?*" (2:3).

Both "for nothing" and "without cause" are forms of the word for grace, *chen*. We see here God is asking Satan why he wants Him to go after Job and cause him harm when he has done nothing to deserve it. Why hurt a man who has done good and not earned the wage of ill-treatment? The list of reasons to inflict pain upon Job is slim, or, "without cause."

Similarly to "nothing", a word derived from *chen* is also translated "free." For example, in Numbers 11:5-6 we read, "We remember the fish which we used to eat *free* in Egypt, the cucumbers and the melons and the leeks and the onions and the garlic, but now our appetite is gone. There is nothing at all to look at except this manna."

The Israelites are so obtuse in the face of God's kindness they look upon the food He has provided for them and label it as "*free.*" The food was hardly "free" since the Israelites were slaves! While they didn't pay money for the food, they paid with their freedom, their uncompensated work, their abuse, and their grief. Yet they are so confused in the wilderness they grumble together, convincing themselves even slavery was better than this journey to the Promised Land, because they had "free" (or "grace") food back there.

Favor

Reminiscent of the original use of *chen* describing Noah's status before God in Genesis, Exodus 33:16 reads, "For how then can it be known that I have found *favor* in Your sight, I and Your people? Is it not by Your going with us, so that we, I and Your people, may be distinguished from all the other people who are upon the face of the earth?" God's favor, or His grace, results in His people "being distinguished," a theme woven throughout the Bible as God calls the Israelites unto Himself as His chosen people, later grafting the Gentiles into the covenant. God chose to set His love, His grace, and His favor upon Moses and the Israelites undeservedly, simply by grace.

America and Grace: Oil and Water?

Grace is a hard concept for many, especially Americans, to comprehend. As a nation full of people whose ethos is one of pulling ourselves up by our bootstraps, working for what we want or need, and making our own way, the concept of grace can often grate on us at best or seem preposterous, even insulting at worst. We want to be able to show our work, to prove we paid for what we've received. But, as elementary as this may sound, God's plan for how He would interact with humanity came along far before American ideology. And while working hard is in many ways a beautiful thing in God's sight, it will never be a means of acquiring right standing with Him. That, beginning with our creation in His image and His breath breathed into our lungs, and someday gloriously concluding with our eternal union with Him, has always been unmerited favor; it is free; it is grace.

This idea of grace as unmerited favor is not seen merely in the Old Testament but in the New Testament as well and seen in Romans 4:4 which reads, "Now to the one who works, his wage is not credited as a *favor*, but that which is due." We see again that grace is the opposite of that which is due. Wages are earned, grace is freely given.

Who Knows?

We're going to look now at an example that is hard to take, as it deals with the death of a child, and found in 2 Samuel 11-12. When King David is meant to be off at war, he instead stays in his palace. He sees a woman, Bathsheba, bathing on her roof (a customary practice), and summons her to him, leveraging his privilege and power to gratify his desires. Sometime after their encounter, Bathsheba notifies David she is pregnant with his child. In a panic to cover his tracks, David quickly arranges to bring home Bathsheba's husband, Uriah, so there will be reason to believe that the baby is his. Uriah reports to David as ordered who dispatches Uriah to his home and wife. Twice Uriah ignores the freedom to see his wife, choosing rather to stay at David's palace in allegiance to his king. Seemingly out of options, David then orders Uriah be placed at the front of the "fiercest battle" where he is killed.

The Lord sends the prophet Nathan to confront David and tells him the child will not live due to David's actions. David repents, weeps, and fasts, asking God for the judgment not to be enacted. The heart of David's prayer is that God may be gracious and not give him what he deserved. But, the child dies, just as the prophet said. Once the child has died, David washes his face, changes his clothes, and no longer appears disheveled. When asked about this transformation, 2 Samuel 12:22 records his answer, "While the child was still alive, I fasted and wept," for I said, "**Who knows** whether the LORD will be *gracious (chen)* to me, that the child may live?"

This is quite convicting. We can be so demanding of God. It is certainly good for believers, whose salvation is secure, to ask and supplicate for that which they desire. But an undemanding spirit shows a much greater understanding of grace than a demanding spirit. When we ask for grace, let us remind ourselves to approach God with an attitude of "who knows?" as David did in his supplication. Let us remember what we are asking for is undeserved, and while God delights to give good gifts, He is not our genie nor compelled to grant our requests.

If You Could Only Have One Section of Scripture

If I were exiled to a desert island and could take just one small section of Scripture with me, it would be Ephesians 2:1-10. The first three verses reveal our terrible plight without God but then 2:4-10 (below) demonstrates His powerful and gracious actions towards us. Read it over slowly, keeping in mind the concepts and word pictures we've been observing around the idea of grace.

"But God, being rich in mercy, because of His great love with which He loved us, even when we were dead in our transgressions, made us alive together with Christ (by *grace [cháris]* you have been saved), and raised us up with Him, and seated us with Him in the heavenly places in Christ Jesus, so that in the ages to come He might show the surpassing riches of His *grace* in kindness toward us in Christ Jesus. For by *grace* you have been saved through faith; and that not of yourselves, it is the gift of God; not as a result of works, so that no one may boast. For we are His workmanship, created in Christ Jesus for good works, which God prepared beforehand so that we would walk in them."

Grace, grace, grace! Paul cannot get enough of God's grace shown to us in Christ. Note the reason the text gives us as to why God made us alive, so He could "**show** the surpassing riches of His *grace* in kindness." It brings God great joy to show us grace—to pour out on us His stunning, ultimate kindness.

The Aaronic Blessing

In closing, let's read the Aaronic Blessing together. This blessing is found in Numbers 6:24-26, and common New Testament greetings of "grace and peace" and "blessing" are most likely sourced in its words. As you read, when you come to the word "gracious", take a moment to substitute some of the concepts and word pictures for grace and see how it illuminates the rest of the passage.

Numbers 6:24-26 says, "The Lord bless you, and keep you; The Lord make His face shine on you, and be *gracious* to you; The Lord lift up His countenance on you, and give you peace."

Grace Lavishly Extended

Of all of God's attributes, God's grace has impacted me the most. Grace was lavishly extended to me, like generous portions at a meal. Grace was lavishly extended to me, providing a model for extending grace toward others. Grace is the absolutely free, unmerited favor of God found in Jesus Christ.

Grace is a game-changer.

Come Thou fount of every blessing, tune my heart to sing Thy grace...

For further study:

Exodus 33:19	Jeremiah 22:13
2 Samuel 24:24	John 1:14-17
Psalm 109:3	Romans 3:24
Proverbs 1:11	Romans 5:15-21
Isaiah 26:10	Romans 6:15; 11:6

CHAPTER 7

GLORY
Kabod | Dóxa

To God be the glory, great things He hath done,
So loved He the world that He gave us His Son,
Who yielded His life an atonement for sin,
And opened the life gate that all may go in.
Praise the Lord, praise the Lord,
Let the earth hear His voice;
Praise the Lord, praise the Lord,
Let the people rejoice;
Oh, come to the Father, through Jesus the Son,
And give Him the glory; great things He hath done.
To God Be The Glory
Fanny J. Crosby

You've got to give a little, take a little,
And let your poor heart break a little.
That's the story of, that's the glory of love.
You've got to laugh a little, cry a little,
Until the clouds roll by a little.
That's the story of, that's the glory of love.
Glory of Love
Billy Hill

The heavens are telling of the glory of God;
And their expanse is declaring the work of His hands.
Psalm 19:1

AS WE HAVE MADE OUR WAY through the stories of our first six words, we have been reminded over and over again how often those of us who are in church settings and Christian subcultures use words we have learned in Scripture and Sunday School without realizing we are unsure of their meanings. And, of course, if those of us who hear them all of the time are not sure of their meanings, then how could those outside of church and Christian contexts possibly have a sense of what we are talking about?

"Glory" is perhaps the poster child for this unfortunate phenomenon. However, it is also a word that has deeply powerful meaning relevant to our everyday lives. For many of us, "glory" may be a word we have only thought about in one dimension, never pondering beyond the fact it's a church/Bible word about God being great in some way. Investigating the Scriptures will reveal a much fuller, three-dimensional understanding for us to recall as we read the Bible, sing worship songs filled with mentions of "glory", and share the good news about Jesus with others in our lives.

In the Old Testament, the word translated "glory" is *kabod*, from the root *kabed*. This term is transliterated and found in the fictional name "Ichabod Crane." In the New Testament, it's *dóxa*, from *dokéō* (to seem, think, recognize). Glory is about what people think about something or someone, i.e., the reputation of the object or person. We see *dóxa* in the term "doxology." Both *kabod* and *dóxa* will carry a consistent concept in both testaments.

It is quite possible of all the words we have studied and will study in this book, "glory", along with being (unfortunately) considered the most one-dimensional, is perhaps (ironically) also the most robust. It is a word pregnant with meaning, and thick with layers for us to discover. We will see it used literally and figuratively, helping us develop a conceptual definition that will work to our benefit both in studying Scripture and going about our modern lives.

Literal Usages of Kabod

The first few examples we are going to look at together are non-theological uses. Remember, "non-theological usages" simply refer to instances in which these words occur in the Bible but don't tell us something directly about God Himself. Rather, they are common, everyday usages of these key words, usages that aid our understanding of the overall concept (or story) of these words.

In 1 Samuel 4:18, we read "When he mentioned the ark of God, Eli fell off the seat backward beside the gate, and his neck was broken and he died, for he was old and *heavy*. Thus he judged Israel forty years." The word for "heavy" here is a form of *kabod*. There is nothing metaphorical or figurative going on in this passage. Eli is a physically large man, and when he falls, the *heaviness* of his body crushes him, breaking his neck. This graphic account provides us with an important part of the key for unlocking the key biblical word "glory." The concept of heaviness, weight, magnitude, is a key component of "glory."

2 Samuel 14:26 shows us a similar usage of *kabod*. It states, "When [Absalom] cut the hair of his head (and it was at the end of every year that he cut it, for it was *heavy* on him so he cut it), he weighed the hair of his head at 200 shekels by the king's weight." Again, we see a form of *kabod* has been translated "heavy", and again it is clear the description here is not figurative or metaphorical. Rather,

it is as practical as can be— Absalom has long hair that is presumably thick and coarse, and the weight of it is so great it becomes heavy upon him.

Figurative Usages of Kabod

As we progress looking at more figurative uses of *kabod*, bear in mind this concept of weight and heaviness. We have seen thus far that "glory" carries the idea of having some weight to it. Glory carries the idea of taking up space, of being sizable and substantive. While the idea of glory will come to mean more to us than that, it will certainly not mean any less.

In the 1960s and '70s, people would often say, "That's heavy!" when conversing about something with great mental or emotional impact. I find this to be a helpful example to remember as I study the idea of "glory." Whether familiar with the Scriptures or not, an entire generation of Americans determined that when something had a profound depth of meaning to it, it was experienced as though it was physically heavy. It was weighty; it was big with meaning; it mattered—it was heavy.

In Ezekiel 21:21 we read, "For the king of Babylon stands at the parting of the way, at the head of the two ways, to use divination; he shakes the arrows, he consults the household idols, he looks at the *liver*." As a bit of historical context, Ezekiel and Daniel are the only two prophets who write during the Babylonian exile (605-539 BC). At this point in history, they are captives in Babylon (modern-day Iraq). Although they have positions in the king's administration, they are still prisoners who cannot leave Babylon and whose Israelite lifestyles and lives are continually threatened.

Ezekiel describes how the King of Babylon makes decisions when determining where to go when a road forks in front of him. He does not seem to consult his rational mind, nor does he defer to the emotional proclivities of his heart. Rather, "He looks at the *liver*." The word "liver" here is the noun *kabed* ("the heavy place"). The liver is the heaviest organ, and many cultures have considered it to be the hub for what we Westerners would call "gut decisions."

So in the mind of the King of Babylon, the liver is the place of heavy and important decisions. This is unlike American culture in which we are more likely to refer to our brains or hearts as the organs we associate with decision-making. Rather than saying, "I feel____" (in my heart) or "I think_____" (in my mind), the king is coming to a decision by consulting what he considers to be the "heaviest" place within himself, the place from which the important decisions are made, and felt.

I distinctly remember teaching this "liver" passage one evening when I was a Bible college professor. The class response was typical—most were initially confused with the idea of "glory" and "liver" being conceptually related, some were beginning to see the idea, and one or two were amazed at the realization. One of the students in the class that night was a missionary on leave from her work in Indonesia. She was so excited she didn't bother to raise her hand but just shouted out, "Now I understand why people in our village sometimes say, 'hati hati!'"

I asked her to clarify and she said in many Indonesian dialects the term "hati" can mean "liver." So, when something important happens (a child wanders too close to the street, exciting news is broken, a mother goes into labor), the cry goes out, "Hati, hati!" or "Liver,

liver!" (or "Weighty, weighty!"). She went on to explain she thought it so strange when people would shout out "Liver, liver!" but this usage in Ezekiel 21 "unlocked" the mystery for her. Something "heavy" is happening! Something "important" is going on!

That's "Heavy" Too

Exodus 8:15 reads, "But when Pharaoh saw that there was relief, he *hardened* (infinite of *kabed* - "to make heavy") his heart and did not listen to them, as the Lord had said." "Hardened" may seem like a bit of a stretch for us to understand at first, but it is, in fact, quite a practical concept. Think of cement as it hardens, becoming a weighty concrete block quite difficult to move or penetrate. This is the image used here. Pharaoh hardened, or, "made heavy" his heart, as though he were adding materials to it to surround and protect it. Pharaoh seeks to make his heart immovable, weighty to the point of permanence, set in his refusal to listen.

Genesis 18:20 says, "And the Lord said, 'the outcry of Sodom and Gomorrah is indeed great, and their sin is exceedingly *grave.*'" While we do not tend to use the word "grave" when we're talking about sin, it is still used at times when discussing medical problems. A doctor or nurse relaying information to a family about a loved one's condition may describe it as "grave." This is common enough medical vernacular that it would tip off most people that the situation is very serious. This situation is big; it's not just going away. It has to be handled.

The translation "grave" also reveals to us that in addition to "glory" conveying the ideas of heaviness, weight, or that which must be handled, it can also reveal the concept of "importance." When someone is facing a chronic, or grave medical condition, this fact suddenly becomes, in a sense, the most important thing about the person at the time. The condition is of such magnitude and priority in the person's life, that it rises to a place of prime importance. Glory then, is an indication of great importance. It is used to describe things or people worth considering important, perceiving as important, and responding to as important.

Genesis 43:1 says, "Now the famine was *severe* (*kabed*) in the land." The crops have not been abundant, or even close to enough, for years and it is affecting everything. Famine is not merely annoying or obtrusive or even just kind of scary; it is of such importance it is affecting the well-being of people's lives. No one, person nor animal, has what they need in terms of food to survive. The famine is of such substance it must be dealt with carefully and quickly. It has, similarly to the sin in Genesis 18:20 when we saw *kabed* translated as "grave", become a weighty matter of such importance and priority that it must be dealt with right now.

Slang Can Be Helpful

Consider some of the slang words used in the past few decades that, at the root, convey the idea of "glory." I shared with you the example of "heavy" from the '60s and '70s, but there are many more words and idioms that have been used to connote the concept of something being so substantive, so weighty in terms of mental or emotional energy, so important, that it has to be discussed or dealt with.

Glory "Slang" List (compiled over the years):
• Heavy
• Phat
• Large

- Deep
- Steep
- Huge
- Mega
- Big deal
- Epic
- Amazing
- Too legit to quit

As silly as it may seem, if one or two of these words stuck out to you, try to keep them in mind as we transition into some of the theological uses of the word *glory* in Scripture. While it may seem a bit strange or even irreverent to think of God as "phat" or "mega", words as part of our common vernacular can help us embed these biblical concepts more deeply than if we attempt to use the common biblical terms. In a sense that is what this book is entirely about. We want to be able to communicate concepts in such a way so that people can remember them, by using words they will find familiar and by helpfully defining the ones they will not. So if you're from the generation that used "heavy" (Buck), or "too legit to quit" (Abby), then bear in mind what those phrases mean or meant as you read of the glory of God.

The Glory of God

Psalm 19:1 reads, "The heavens are telling of the *glory* (*kabod*) of God; and their expanse is declaring the work of His hands." This verse is so brief and reads so simply, yet it bears so much within its few words. The heavens, the huge expanse God separated from the waters below on the second day of creation, that massive space is declaring the enormity of God. It is telling us how (to use one of our slang words) "epic" He is, how in charge and powerful He is, how He must be dealt with before anything else truly can be.

God is the One around Whom our lives must be arranged. The heavens are inviting us, the psalmist is saying, to consider just how important God is, just how many important things He has made, does make, and will make happen. Psalm 86:9-12 states:

> "All nations whom You have made shall…worship before You, O Lord,
> And they shall *glorify* (*kabed*) Your name.
> For You are great and do wondrous deeds;
> You alone are God.
> Teach me Your way, O Lord;
> I will walk in Your truth;
> Unite my heart to fear Your name.
> I will give thanks to You, O Lord my God, with all my heart,
> And will *glorify* (*kabed*) Your name forever."

Like the prior psalm we discussed, this passage so beautifully reminds us to ponder the acts of God and say, "Look! Look at what He has done and what this must mean about Him. Look upon the One Who made this universe and has done great things. How important, How wonderful, How great and worthy of our priorities He must be." The psalmist articulates here what we are called to coach our hearts in believing and doing—God truly is as great as He and His creation tell us He is. Let us, therefore, respond to Him as such.

New Testament Glory

The New Testament has no shortage of passages referencing glory, specifically in the letters of Paul. 2

Corinthians 4:17, for example, reads "for momentary, light affliction is producing for us an eternal *weight of glory* far beyond all comparison." In this verse, Paul hits us with a double dose by using a Greek term for "weight" (*baros*) as well as *dóxa* ("glory"). This suffering we feel now on earth, though it can be incredibly painful and full of genuine grief, is not for nothing. When endured by the grace of God, it is creating an unimaginably important reward that will not merely anesthetize the pain we have felt on this side of eternity, but, for lack of a better phrase, blow our minds entirely with its goodness, its importance, its heaviness.

Ephesians 1:6, 12, and 14 state, "To the praise of the *glory (dóxa)* of His grace, which He freely bestowed on us in the Beloved...that we who were the first to hope in Christ would be to the praise of His *glory*...with a view to the redemption of God's own possession, to the praise of His *glory*." Here, Paul is quite intent his readers do not miss this fact—the gracious salvation of man points to the glory, the magnitude, the greatness, the importance, of God. Both a testament and a credit to God's unimaginable grace on our behalf, the glory of our salvation is found fully in what it says about Who God is, and what He is willing to do so that man might be saved.

Let us consider one more common phrase that may help us understand the biblical concept of glory a bit more clearly. The phrase is "blow it off." I often work with college students, and, as part of our discussions, we will sometimes go over their weekly class schedules. They will tell me about the courses that require a great deal of attention as well as the ones they can "blow off." The reason they, and I (and maybe you) use the phrase "blow it off," is that we have assigned a "lightness" to the topic or issue at hand. It seems so light in our minds that just our breath can move it aside, indicating we aren't giving the topic much attention, much weight. But then there are those classes, or those projects, or those opportunities, or those people that the students (and you and I) arrange their lives around—those, of course, are the heavy ones, the important ones, the "glorious" ones.

In Romans 3:23 we read, "For all have sinned and fall short of the *glory* (*dóxa*) of God." Recall from an earlier chapter that to sin is to do what? To miss the mark or standard. Those who have sinned (all of us) are those who have missed the mark of assessing God's glory for what it is. We have failed to see His importance, His heaviness, His must-be-dealt-with-ness, for what it is. We have sinned; we fall short of recognizing His importance and responding to it in kind. Only by His Son Jesus Christ can we perfectly hit the mark and be restored to meeting the standard of righteousness, of responding correctly to the glory of God.

Wrapping Up

When you are reading Scripture and you come across the word *glory*, ask yourself if the usage is figurative or literal. Is this telling me someone is physically large? Is it telling me someone's hair is long and weighs him down? Or is it telling me something is of great importance? The key to unlocking this key biblical word is asking yourself those questions while consistently recalling the concepts of heavy, important, must be dealt with (perhaps even "steep" or "epic") in your interpretations.

The Westminster Shorter Catechism states, "Man's chief end is to glorify God, and to enjoy Him forever." So what does it mean to "glorify" the Lord? We cannot make God more glorious than He is, but we can make his glory (importance) known to others. To glorify God is to ascribe honor and importance to the One Who is all glorious, all-important, Who dwells in glory.

As you continue to ponder this word and its usages in Scripture, consider how your life can be a testament to God's importance. What would it look like to consider God's glory this week? What intentional steps can you make to rearrange the various components of your life around His central presence, His importance? As you seek to make Him known and respond to Him in recognition of His ultimate importance, you will be glorifying Him just as the psalmists and Paul did, and now do, in His presence.

For further study:

Genesis 13:2	Psalm 50:23
Exodus 20:12	Isaiah 58:13
Exodus 33:18, 22	Ezekiel 3:5-6
1 Samuel 4:18-5:11	John 1:14, 2:1

CHAPTER 8

HOLY
Qodesh | Hágios

Holy, holy, holy
Lord God almighty
Early in the morning my song shall rise to thee
Holy, holy, holy
Merciful and mighty
God in three persons, blessed Trinity.
Holy, Holy, Holy
Reginald Heber

When I was a boy, each week
On Sunday, we would go to church
And pay attention to the priest
He would read the holy word
And consecrate the holy bread
And everyone would kneel and bow
Today the only difference is
Everything is holy now
Everything, everything
Everything is holy now.
Holy Now
Peter Mayer

Seraphim stood above Him, each having six wings: with
two he covered his face, and with two he covered his feet,
and with two he flew. And one called out to another and
said, "Holy, Holy, Holy, is the Lord of hosts,
the whole earth is full of His glory."
Isaiah 6:2-3

HOLY MAY BE THE MOST MISUNDERSTOOD word we are attempting to unlock in this book. We tend to think of holy as connoting merely the idea of sinlessness, but there is, just as with all our key words, a much greater narrative revealed when the word's various usages are fully investigated. Some of the instances we will see in Scripture are likely to be quite surprising, but hang with it. When we are able to understand the concept of holiness in its broader biblical context, a more robust definition we can keep with us in future studies of Scripture will be its own reward.

In the Old Testament, the common Hebrew word for "holy" is *qodesh* (from the root verb *qadash*). In the New Testament, the word is *hágios*. In short, the words *qodesh* and *hágios* will convey the idea of something or someone being set apart or distinct. Other helpful words and phrases to bear in mind are:

Not common
Special
Apartness
Sacred
Consecrated

Wholly Other

Another way to think of "holy" comes from the idea of "wholly" other, which will require a bit of explaining. First, it's a helpful wordplay between "holy" and "wholly." The key is to think through the concept of "whole," a descriptor conveying ideas such as "entirely; completely; all of." The idea here is when God is described as holy, it's like He is almost alien in comparison to humanity in that He is "completely other."

While we are a little bit like God, since we are made in His image, God is, in His essence, entirely different from us. Jesus is not just a good one of us. As we read Scripture and contemplate the various uses of the words for holy, consider how understanding God as holy can actually draw us closer to Him, rather than push us away from Him as we may first think. It's easy to wonder, "Well, if God is nothing like me, doesn't that mean my chances for being near Him are smaller?" But because our God is so good, He sent His Son to be like us, so we may be brought near to Him Who is holy, Who is wholly other. As Third Day sang, "God of wonders beyond our galaxy. You are holy, holy."[2]

As we progress, consider the ongoing definition of "holy" as that which (or he/she whom) is set apart, distinct, special. We will fill out those definitions and concepts as we analyze several verses together.

Interestingly, our language is filled with usages of the word holy. Here is a list I've collected over years from teaching these word studies in classrooms and asking students for their examples:

Holy Smoke	Holy Land
Holy Moses	Holy Bread
Holy Toledo	Holy Grail
Holy Cow	Holy Ghost
Holy Mackerel	Holy Bible
Holy Moly	Holy Spirit
Holy Cannoli	Holy City
Holy Macaroni	Holy Cross
Holy Molinga (personal favorite!)	Holy Joe
Holy Guacamole	Holy of Holies
Holy Schnikees	Holy Water
Holy Cats	Holy War

[2] Marc Byrd and Steven Hindalong. *God of Wonders*. Universal Music Publishing Group, Capitol Christian Music Group, 2004.

Holy Friday	Holy Roller
Holy Week	Holy Matrimony
Holy Night	Holi-day

As you read, and likely smile at a few, consider if you ever use these phrases or other variations. What does it mean to you when you use the word holy? Bear this question in mind as we move on from this exercise and reflect upon how Scripture incorporates the word "holy."

While we may not often use the word "holy," the concept is certainly found in our culture. The china collection we bring out only for Christmas? Holy dishes. The guest room towels not to be touched by the kids? Holy linens. The restaurant visited only on anniversaries? Holy dining. The days in our year that commemorate special events or people? Holi-days.

Now that we've gotten into the "what does holy really mean and why do we use it?" mindset, let's look at some non-theological uses of the words.

Ordinary or Special Bread?

In 1 Samuel 21:1-6 we read, "Then David came to Nob to Ahimelech the priest; and Ahimelech came trembling to meet David and said to him, 'Why are you alone and no one with you?' David said to Ahimelech the priest, 'The king has commissioned me with a matter and has said to me, 'Let no one know anything about the matter on which I am sending you and with which I have commissioned you; and I have directed the young men to a certain place.' Now therefore, what do you have on hand? Give me five loaves of bread, or whatever can be found.' The priest answered David and said, 'There is no **ordinary** bread on hand, but there is *consecrated* bread; if only the young men have kept themselves from women.'

David answered the priest and said to him, 'Surely women have been kept from us as previously when I set out and the vessels of the young men were *holy*, though it was an **ordinary** journey; how much more then today will their vessels be *holy*?' So the priest gave him *consecrated* bread..."

In these verses, we see four usages of *qodesh* ("consecrated" twice and "holy" twice). However, the key to understanding *qodesh* here is the use of the term "ordinary" (*chol*), also found twice in this section. The structure reveals them to be antonyms. Holy is the opposite of ordinary! Holy is that which is special!

For the men to be qualified to receive the bread reserved for use in the tabernacle, Ahimelech the priest first needed to ensure the young men were ritually clean ("kept themselves from women") and therefore eligible to eat the consecrated bread. David argues even though they were on an "ordinary" journey the men were "holy" (as they have been kept from women) and therefore the consecrated (or special) bread should be theirs to have. For our purposes, the point of the passage is merely the difference between ordinary and holy, between common and uncommon.

A Special Altar

Exodus 29:37 reads, "For seven days you shall make atonement for the altar and consecrate it; then the altar shall be most *holy* (*qodesh*), and whatever touches the altar shall be *holy* (*qodesh*)." The altar's need for atonement did not indicate the altar had a moral problem. The altar, as an inanimate object, does not have a capacity for morality. Rather, because the altar was the place where God met His people, it must be seen (or considered) as "holy"—special, consecrated, different from the norm.

The molecular constitution of the rocks that form the altar did not change, but the seven days of "altar atonement" caused the altar to be made special in the minds of the worshippers, making it a distinct place, appropriate for the sacrifice of atonement. The altar is rendered to be out of the ordinary, special, or holy.

A Special Day

Although I think all seven days of the creation week should be included in Genesis Chapter 1, it is likely the editors drew the break where they did to show the specialness of the Sabbath day. In Genesis 2:3 we read, "Then God blessed the seventh day and *sanctified* (*qodesh*) it, because in it He rested from all His work which God had created and made."

When God blessed the seventh day, He "sanctified" it—He made it holy. This day is made holy by the fact God did not do what He had ordinarily done for the six days prior, rather He rested, which is out of the ordinary, or holy. God set aside a holy time, a distinct day for observing and enjoying what He has made. This day is not a day in which He created; it is not a day when He caused flowers to burst from the ground or fish to appear in the sea or birds to fly through the air. This day is something else; it is marked by difference; it is holy.

It is fascinating to note how some Jewish people observe the Sabbath Day in modern times. If you visit Jerusalem or certain neighborhoods in New York City, you may notice wires or lines stretched between poles somewhat high up overhead. These wires form enclosures known as "eruvim" (also "eruvin" or "eruvs") so Orthodox Jews may know how far they can and cannot walk on the Sabbath according to Rabbinical Law. This is one way they quantify the difference between work and rest in an attempt to follow the model God demonstrated by working for six days and resting on the seventh.

A Special Prostitute?

In Genesis 38:21-22 we read, "He [Judah, by way of his friend] asked the men of her place, saying, 'Where is the *temple prostitute* who was by the road at Enaim?' But they said, 'There has been no *temple prostitute* here.' So he returned to Judah, and said, 'I did not find her; and furthermore the men of the place said, 'There has been no *temple prostitute* here.'" Three times the Hebrew uses *qedesah*, the feminine form of our term for "holy" (*qodesh*) to describe a female prostitute. What in the world is going on here?

In this passage, Judah sends his friend to look for the woman he (Judah) was with recently as described in Genesis 38:12-19, but she is nowhere to be found. This is because she was, in fact, his daughter-in-law, Tamar, who is described to be a "temple prostitute."[3] As the Israelite faith became devastatingly syncretistic, the practice of temple prostitution became more common. People believed through sexual union with a temple prostitute, they were uniting more completely with the deity the temple prostitute represented. There were also common prostitutes in these times, those who were not solicited for the sake of worship. But the temple prostitutes were thought of as the special ones, the holy ones. Tamar

---

[3] In fairness, Genesis 38:15 first describes the woman as a "harlot" (*zona*), so Judah's friend may have been elevating her social status in the eyes of those he encountered. Or Moses may have been "thickening the plot" a bit for the reader, slowly revealing the special nature of this "harlot." For our purposes, neither one of these possibilities really matters as the term *qedesah* is used three times to describe her. What is a *qedesah*?

(probably veiled to protect her identity) pretended not to be a common prostitute, but a temple prostitute, a special one connected to the worship of a god. There are other references to temple prostitution in Deuteronomy 23:17; 1 Kings 14:24; 15:12; 22:46; 2 Kings 23:7; Job 36:14.

It is likely I have just entirely ruined your idea of what "holy" means, and in a sense, I'm sorry. The purpose, though, is to show that holy does not mean sinless—it means set apart or distinct. It means someone or something is special, it is not common.

A Special God

We will turn now to a few theological usages of *qodesh* and *hágios* to see how they are used to describe God.

Isaiah 6:3 reads, "In the year of King Uzziah's death I saw the Lord sitting on a throne, lofty and exalted, with the train of His robe filling the temple. Seraphim stood above Him, each having six wings: with two he covered his face, and with two he covered his feet, and with two he flew. And one called out to another and said, '*Holy*, *Holy*, *Holy*, is the Lord of hosts, the whole earth is full of His glory.'"

"Holy, Holy, Holy"—this Lord is special, distinct, not ordinary. He is the ruler of this multitude of armies; the whole earth is full of His importance. So special, so distinct, so uncommon, was the King before Isaiah that he was overcome to the point of only being able to say the word he knew to mean special, set apart, and distinct over and over again—"Holy! Holy! Holy!" The whole earth is full of His glory!

In Luke 5:8, we see Peter's response to Jesus filling fishing nets so full the boats begin to sink. He replies, "But when Simon Peter saw that, he fell down at Jesus' feet, saying, 'Go away from me Lord, for I am a sinful man!'" In the presence of the special uncommonness of Jesus, Peter becomes acutely aware of the starkness of his base commonality. It's like being dressed in a dirty old tee shirt with tattered shorts and entering a Black tie wedding ceremony. All of a sudden, a difference has been made clear. Starkly clear.

Revelation 4:8 reads, "And the four living creatures, each one of them having six wings, are full of eyes around and within; and day and night they do not cease to say, '*Holy, holy, holy* is the Lord God, the Almighty, who was and who is and who is to come.'" Shortly after this in verse ten, we read of the 24 elders who repeatedly fall down before "Him Who sits on the throne." I like to refer to this as the "falling down ministry" in which the mantra is, "It is not right that I stand when you are sitting on the throne." The elders, in response to the living creatures' profession of God's holiness, use their bodies to say to God, "I should be beneath You and different from You so to acknowledge Your difference, Your specialness, Your set-apartness, Your holiness."

In 1 Peter 1:16 and Leviticus 11:44-45 we read, "For I am the Lord your God. *Consecrate* yourselves therefore, and be *holy*; for I am *holy*...For I am the Lord, who brought you up from the land of Egypt, to be your God; thus you shall be *holy* for I am *holy*." Do you see here what God is saying to us? Let us not just be holy in our actions! Rather, may we be conformed to the image of Christ's identity and character. May our holy actions be an outflow of a holy essence and identity, rooted in the character of God, made possible only by the person of Jesus Christ, and fueled by the Holy Spirit.

It's More Than Just Sinning Less!

To think of holiness as merely sinning less is to miss the point. The idea behind holiness, whether theologically or non-theologically, is that which is distinct and special, not ordinary. For the Christian, the holiness of God is an invitation to participate in the process of being made holy, from the inside out. As Tim Keller said, "If Jesus became incarnate to live among the ordinary, then what we call ordinary is really special to God."[4]

Dance with Him!

Don't sit out the dance! You have the chance to be involved in being set apart by living a life pleasing to God. May we remember how differently God sees us, and may we make choices in our every day lives that acknowledge just how special and distinct He is.

Words and phrases to ponder:
• Saints = holy ones; Paul's typical greeting in his letters to believers who are considered special/holy because of their relationship with God through Christ
• Sanctify/sanctification = becoming holy
• Holi-day = a special day
• Halloween = All Saints ("Holy") Eve
• "Hallowed" be thy name = God's name is special
• "Hallowed" ground = special battlefield or graveyard

For further study:

Deuteronomy 22:9	Ezekiel 36:20-23
Nehemiah 12:47	1 Corinthians 1:2 and most of Paul's greetings
Jeremiah 12:3	

---

[4] Keller, Timothy (@timkellernyc); May 3, 2015

CHAPTER 9

LOVINGKINDNESS
Hesed

Baby, what say we stay together
Let's start with loving kindness
And leave no room for hurt
And when times get hard and we want to give up
Baby, what say we stay together?
What Say
George Strait

Here is love, vast as the ocean
Lovingkindness as the flood
When the Prince of Life, our Ransom
Shed for us His precious blood
Who His love will not remember?
Who can cease to sing His praise?
He can never be forgotten
Throughout Heaven's eternal days.
Here Is Love
William Rees

Surely my soul remembers
And is bowed down within me.
This I recall to my mind,
Therefore I have hope.
The Lord's lovingkindnesses indeed never cease,
For His compassions never fail.
They are new every morning;
Great is Your faithfulness.
Lamentations 3:21-23

WHILE THE OTHER WORDS WE HAVE STUDIED have fallen within a range from foreign to familiar, both to church and unchurched people, "lovingkindness" is likely to be planted firmly alongside the boundary marker labeled "foreign." People with little to no faith background find themselves using the word "helper" all the time, or they may have an abstract understanding of the concepts of "sin" and "holy." While the Bible presents much fuller definitions of each of those words, that little bit of familiarity, even if not entirely correct, can often be found somewhere in the "rarely used vocabulary" file of most English-speakers' minds.

The same cannot be said, though, for the word "lovingkindness," can it? While "loving" and "kindness" are familiar to most, the compound word "lovingkindness" sounds like, well, a compound word that means, well, I'm not sure what it means! But is it more than simply two words smushed together? I think as we study several instances of "lovingkindness" in Scripture, we'll find it is, in fact, much more.

The Hebrew word for lovingkindness is *hesed* (or *chesed*). Except for a camp counselor of Abby's whose name was "Kesi" in homage to *hesed* or a reference to a *Hasidic* Jew, *hesed* is a rare term in English. There is no Greek word that serves as a direct correlate to *hesed*. However, many times in the NT, as well as in hymns and modern songs that espouse the characteristics of God, the use of "faithfulness" is intended to conjure up similar ideas to "lovingkindness." Remember, "faith" in Hebrew is *aman*, from which we get the English word "amen," meaning, "let it be so." When we pray, we are asking God what we have prayed to become so. We are asking Him to move on our behalf in accord with His faithfulness, in keeping with His lovingkindness.

Love is a Choice

Inherent to God's love is the concept of choice. While this may seem like a distinct theological opinion, try not to think of it quite that narrowly. In this chapter, all I mean by "inherent to God's love is the concept of choice" is this—God does not express love on a whim or based on shifting feelings toward humanity at any given moment. Rather, God chooses to love. He sets His affection. How does God choose to interact with humanity? He chooses to love. While its expressions vary and may not always look like our idea of love, Scripture is clear. God decides to love His image-bearers.

Love and Hate

One of the more uncomfortable instances of this truth in Scripture occurs in Malachi 1:2-3 (as quoted in Romans 9:13) when God says, "I loved Jacob, but I have hated Esau." The idea of God "hating" someone does not sit well with us and our Western understanding of what it is to love or hate. We tend to only see those terms as expressions of emotion. But this passage is telling us God did not choose Esau to be the father of the Israelites, while He did choose Jacob to be the father of the Israelites (and in the chosen lineage of the Messiah). Jacob He chose; Esau He did not choose. Jacob He loved; Esau He hated.

Towards a Definition

God's love is a choice. The emotion or feeling of love is never the lead horse when it comes to God's love. As counterintuitive as this may seem, let it be an encouragement to you rather than a discouragement. It is not that God does not have great feelings of love for you. Rather, His love is immovable, set upon His children, and from this determined love comes feelings and expressions of love.

Remember, our rough New Testament equivalent for lovingkindness is faithfulness. God remains committed to us even when we rebel against Him, even when He would have, to our human minds, every right to walk away from us in our selfishness. But He is faithful; He exercises lovingkindness. In a relationship where one has chosen to love another, kindness is found.

Lovingkindness is loyal, enduring covenantal love within any kind of relational agreement. It is not necessarily legal, though it can be, but it is any kind of **loyal love**. By invoking lovingkindness, one is stating, "I will be loyal to you in my choice of you." When it comes to God, lovingkindness is an impenetrable determined faithfulness. It is the "glue" of God. God's lovingkindness is His vow to stick to what He has said. Once He has vowed His lovingkindness, the manifestation of it is not dependent upon the behavior of the one with whom He has made a covenant. Behavior that honors God is (obviously) desired, but it is not essential to the loyalty of the Covenant Maker.

As we begin to peruse the Scriptures for usages of "lovingkindness," keep this working definition in your mind. Lovingkindness is determined faithfulness, a loyalty that sticks regardless of what may come. It is a covenant of love.

Hesed Lesson #1 from Jonathan and David

In 1 Samuel 18-20, we see King Saul's anger and jealousy had reached the boiling point. David's prowess on the battlefield and popularity with the people were too much for Saul to handle. In Chapters 18 and 19, Saul twice attempted (unsuccessfully) to kill David with a spear. In

Chapter 20, Saul's spear was directed at his son, Jonathan, who had befriended David against his father's command. The friendship of Jonathan and David was special, a pact sealed with *hesed* as 1 Samuel 20:12-17 beautifully described their last meeting and the following conversation.

"Then Jonathan said to David, 'The Lord, the God of Israel, be witness! When I have sounded out my father about this time tomorrow, or the third day, behold, if there is good feeling toward David, shall I not then send to you and make it known to you? If it please my father to do you harm, may the Lord do so to Jonathan and more also, if I do not make it known to you and send you away, that you may go in safety. And may the Lord be with you as He has been with my father. If I am still alive, will you not show me the *lovingkindness (hesed)* of the Lord, that I may not die? And you shall not cut off your *lovingkindness (hesed)* from my house forever, not even when the Lord cuts off every one of the enemies of David from the face of the earth.' So Jonathan made a covenant with the house of David, saying, 'May the Lord require it at the hands of David's enemies.' Jonathan made David vow again because of his love for him, because he loved him as he loved his own life."

Jonathan is not merely asking for human loyalty to be prioritized in his relationship with David. Rather, he is asking David to invoke God's lovingkindness in their relationship, not only their relationship as individuals, but with the "house of David." David is going to be king soon, and his "house," which can be understood both as his lineage and all who work within his administration, will be of great importance in maintaining this covenant that invokes the lovingkindness of God.

The Bible has a maddening habit of assuming you know the Bible. It assumes you have paid attention to what it has been said up to the point you are reading. It often reflects on accounts previously told, and it trusts your understanding of God's character and how He interacts with humanity is growing as you read. There is a great deal that can be learned by reading just one account in Scripture, to be sure, but there is a great deal more that can be missed (or misinterpreted) if individual accounts are not understood within the broader context of what has led up to that specific moment.

Hesed Lesson #2 from Jonathan and David

Bearing in mind David and Jonathan's covenant in 1 Samuel 20, let's move forward to some helpful usages of *hesed* as seen in 2 Samuel 9. There is an important change that has occurred in Israel. David is now king. It was common in those days, as it has been throughout much of world history, for the new king to demand everyone who was related to or identified with the prior king be removed from places of power and in some instances, even be killed. When a new administration took over, to ensure personnel and policies were not threatened, it systematically removed anyone whose loyalty may lead them to be insubordinate or dangerous. Whether one sees it as brutal or wise to displace those who could be of harm to a new administration, it is simply the way things have been for much of history.

And so as we arrive at 2 Samuel 9, David is king. Saul and Jonathan have died, though members of the house of Saul still remain. Remember, Saul had thrown a spear at David years before this. It would have been expected David would kill, or at least banish, any members of the house of Saul. Yet rather than seeking vengeance upon anyone who was part of the house of Saul, David makes an inquiry of another kind entirely. He asks in 9:1, "Is there yet anyone left of the house of Saul, that I may show him *kindness* for Jonathan's sake?" A servant of the house named Ziba informs David there is still a son of Jonathan, Mephibosheth, who is "crippled in both feet." David sends for Mephibosheth and says to him in 9:7, "I will surely show *kindness* to you for the sake of your father Jonathan...you shall eat at my table regularly." In this section, *hesed* is translated "kindness."

Perhaps the table where David welcomed Mephibosheth to eat with him was the same table where David had sat at dinners with Saul and Jonathan many years before. Perhaps it was the same table at which Jonathan had dodged his father's spear. What we do know is this—at that exact moment in David's reign as king, there was no more physically and essentially vulnerable person than Mephibosheth, one who literally cannot run. Yet David does not lord his strength over Mephibosheth's weakness. He does not respond to him based on ability, according to behavior, or in proportion to what Mephibosheth had to offer David. Rather, David does to Mephibosheth according to the covenant he made with his father, Jonathan, the covenant David now intends to keep. He shows *hesed*. Notice the difference in human relationships *hesed* can make. A determination of loyalty transforms how we relate to one another, which we see most fully in the character of God and how He relates to us.

Hesed Lesson from Joshua and the Gibeonites

Later in 2 Samuel 21, there is a famine recorded. Though this account occurs towards the end of 2 Samuel, remember, the Bible assumes you know the Bible. Critical to understanding 2 Samuel 21 is Deuteronomy 28, where we observe a motif of blessing and cursing revealed in the Mosaic covenant. "Motif" makes it sound fancy and complicated; all it means is God has a "design" for his relationship with the Israelites that if they keep the Law of Moses, life will generally go well with them, and if they do not, it won't. According to Deuteronomy 28, famine was an indicator Israel was not keeping the Law.

So when we begin to inspect the details of 2 Samuel 21 we see a three-year famine is occurring, which would roughly be equivalent to a three-year bear market in our modern economic lingo. Or, perhaps an increasingly severe shortage of fruits and vegetables at the grocery store, such that things were becoming quite concerning. So, it should perk up our ears a little. Something is very wrong. Things are not going well for the Israelites.

2 Samuel 21:1 states, "The Lord said, 'It (the famine) is for Saul and his bloody house, because he put the Gibeonites to death.'" However, there is no reference in 1 or 2 Samuel of Saul killing Gibeonites. What in the world is going on? But there is a reference to the Gibeonites way back in the book of Joshua. Let's check it out.

Joshua had been given an order from God to kill anyone who was in the way of the Israelites on their quest to the Promised Land. Sin was so rampant and influenced the Israelites so heavily God determined their enemies should be wholly destroyed. Joshua is obeying God's command and militarily eliminating all who are in the way of the Israelites.

Joshua 9 reports the Gibeonites learned of this plan. They realize they are surrounded by the Israelites, determine they cannot defeat them militarily, but decide to try to outsmart them. So the Gibeonites dress in dirty, torn clothes, allow their bread to become dry and crumbled, and present themselves to Joshua as no threat whatsoever. They present their case to Joshua, stating they are merely passing through the land and mean the Israelites no harm. Faced with this apparent ethical dilemma, Joshua does not consult the Lord. Rather, he makes a covenant with the Gibeonites to become bondservants of the Israelites, thus allowing them to live. Joshua and the leaders swear this covenant to the Gibeonites "by the Lord." In essence, they swear the *hesed* of Yahweh over the pact.

Now, go back to 2 Samuel 21, some 400 years later. (Remember the maddening little truism—the Bible assumes you know the Bible.) Saul and his "bloody house" had killed some Gibeonites sometime during his reign as king (although the details of the event are not recorded in Scripture). The covenant made by Joshua and sworn to the Gibeonites "by the Lord" continued to stand even toward the end of David's kingship, some 400 years later! The ramifications of the pact broken by Saul now rest upon David. The *hesed* of the Lord is not eroded by time.

So David, bound by a pact made by Joshua four centuries prior, is forced to bring justice against the house of Saul. David determines seven of Saul's male descendants (two sons, five grandsons) must be executed to atone for Saul's sin. Wait, does this include Mephibosheth? 2 Samuel 21:7 records the answer to the question—"but the king spared Mephibosheth, the son of Jonathan the son of Saul, because of the oath of the LORD which was between them, between David and Saul's son Jonathan." At the core of the oath was *hesed*, the endurable glue of the covenant made between Jonathan and David back in 1 Samuel 20!

Hesed is Serious Business

God is serious about commitments made in His name. When we invoke His lovingkindness into our human relationships, we are bringing Him in as a "co-covenanter." He does not forget that to which His name has been attached. Marriage covenants, pacts made "in the name of God," are serious. God has been brought into the covenant as a third party.

Other Hesed Lessons

In Hosea 6:4-6, we read,

> "What shall I do with you, O Ephraim?
> What shall I do with you, O Judah?
> For your *loyalty* is like a morning cloud
> And like the dew which goes away early.
> Therefore I have hewn them in pieces by the prophets;
> I have slain them by the words of My mouth;
> And the judgments on you are like the light that goes forth.
> For I delight in *loyalty* rather than sacrifice,
> And in the knowledge of God rather than burnt offerings."

Ephraim, the largest of the ten northern tribes, is used here to represent all of Israel. At first, God's description of their loyalty (*hesed*) seems lovely. Morning clouds, sprinkled dew—what a nice image! But just a few hours later, where are those morning clouds, where is the dew? It is gone. When the heat comes, it does not stick around. The loyalty of the Israelites was empty, it didn't last. God is saying, "You claim to have loyalty, but you don't really. You can't take the heat."

In English, Micah 7:18-20 translates *hesed* as "unchanging love." Micah is reminding the Israelites the God Who loves them is true to His Word, and He loves it. He loves righteousness, He loves loyalty, and those facts simply do not change.

In Lamentations 3:21-24, Jeremiah writes of God's lovingkindness. The prophet has just seen the fall of his nation's capital. Everything is destroyed, yet he states, "This I recall to mind, therefore I have hope. The Lord's *lovingkindnesses* (*hesed*) indeed never cease, for His compassions never fail. They are new every morning; great is Thy faithfulness. The Lord is my portion, says my soul, therefore I have hope in Him."

What is there to recall in tragedy? The Lord's lovingkindness. We must have this truth hidden deep within us **before** the tragedy strikes. We must ask the Scriptures—how does God act? What does God care about? When tragedy strikes, a deep knowledge of God rooted in the words of the Bible offers us a deep comfort.

In 2 Timothy 2:11-13, we read, "It is a trustworthy statement: For if we died with Him, we will also live with Him; if we endure, we will also reign with Him. If we deny Him, He also will deny us; if we are faithless, He remains faithful, for He cannot deny Himself."

The "formula" seen in verses 11-12 changes in the last line, doesn't it? Consistency would have it read, "If we are faithless; He will be faithless." But God cannot deny Himself; He swore an oath. The blood of God, the insignia of God, seals the covenant. Why would I want to be anywhere other than with Him? To Whom shall I go if not You? No circumstance will violate His oath to us. This is heart-melting. His *hesed* calls us to stick with Him as we know He will stick with us!

The final verse of Psalm 23 in the old King James Version begins with the stanza, "Surely goodness and *mercy* will follow me all the days of my life." For years, I was under the impression the word for "mercy" here was the rather common term *kippur* (as in Yom *Kippur* or the Day of Atonement), a form of the Hebrew *kaphar* ("to cover over"). But it is *hesed*. Lovingkindness will follow the psalmist all the days of his life, because God has made an oath, and He is the best oath-er there is, the One Who makes unbreakable oaths. The "glue of God" sticks to us. It follows us all the days our lives!

Final Thoughts on Hesed

Lovingkindness expresses a sweet determination to enjoy the love of a relationship, through the setting of the will. It is a loyal, enduring love, a determined faithfulness, the kindness exhibited in a loyal relationship. It is a setting of love, which can occur even in circumstances that seem extreme to Western thought, like arranged marriages. Juxtapose determined love with the account of Samson who tells his parents a woman looks good to him, "So go get her for me," or David who sends for Bathsheba because she looks good to him. These are the fulfilling of lusts, rather than the setting of love. Lovingkindness calls us to a setting of the will for the betterment of the beloved.

For further study:

Deuteronomy 7:9-12	Psalm 136 - every verse!
Nehemiah 13:14	Isaiah 40:6-8
Psalm 115:1	

CHAPTER 10

COMPASSION
Rachamim | Splágchnon

I used to think love was a dying art
Compassion couldn't live within a crowded heart
I saw my freedom in a poor man's eyes
Hope like a light, will to survive
A sense of dignity to hold up high
These are the simple things
That keep us all alive
And though the rich buy power for a time
One thing that money can't buy.
Love & Compassion Lyrics
Hall & Oates

What boundless love,
What fathomless grace
You have shown us, O God of compassion!
Each day we live
An offering of praise
As we show to the world Your compassion.
Compassion Hymn
Keith & Kristyn Getty

Be gracious to me, O God,
according to Your lovingkindness;
According to the greatness of Your compassion
blot out my transgressions.
Psalm 51:1

WHAT DOES THE WORD "COMPASSION" bring to your mind? You may think of something akin to pity, or of a large nonprofit organization that offers aid to children in developing countries. You may think of compassion as a personality trait—a tendency toward caring for people who are hurting which some people may have and some may not. Or you may put it in the same camp as "grace" and "mercy," thinking of it as a certain posture God has toward humanity, or that which humans can have toward one another.

In Hebrew, the word for compassion is often rendered *rachamim,* the plural of *rechem.* In Greek, it is *splágchnon.* In the OT, *rachamim* often conveys a collective sense with the word *hesed* we studied in the previous chapter, often translated as "lovingkindness." When we see various passages in Scripture include the word "compassion," we will often see "lovingkindness" nearby. They pair together nicely.

Lessons from the Womb

The common Hebrew word for "womb" is *rechem.* The plural form is our word *rachamim,* or "wombs" (literally!). In Hebrew, the plural is often used to convey the idea of fullness. So, the concept is more like "the fullness of the womb" or "the full expression of the womb."

What is, then, the full expression of the womb? When a mother is pregnant with her child, she is filled with the desire to prevent any distress from befalling the child of her womb. And this desire does not end when her child is no longer in her womb. Rather, even as he or she is born, grows up, and becomes an adult, the "full expression of the womb," though it may manifest differently, lives on.

Recall our study of the word "glory" and the Ezekiel 21 passage when the King of "looked to the liver" to make a decision? The idea of understanding compassion as "womb" is a similar concept to understanding glory as "liver." The womb is the place where a "gut feeling" is housed—a feeling that is deep, essential, and compels one to act on behalf of another.

As we begin to consider biblical usages of the words for compassion, keep the concept of "womb" in mind, as well as "the fullness of the womb." One who experiences the feeling of compassion is one who has a desire to aid the distressed. One who experiences "the fullness of the womb" has a tender feeling in their womb for someone special to them, or from their womb.

By the way, this does not have to be literal. Men, of course, do not have wombs, but they still experience feelings of deep compassion (as the Scriptures will show us). One for whom you have deep affection, one for whom you experience tender feelings of mercy and desire to act for their good, is a person whom you could think of as being from your "womb."

Human Compassion

Let's consider some non-theological usages of *rechem* and *rachamim*.

In Genesis 29:31 we read, "Now the Lord saw that Leah was unloved, and He opened her *womb*, but Rachel was barren." Similarly, 1 Samuel 1:5 states, "But to Hannah he would give a double portion, for he loved Hannah, but the Lord had closed her *womb*." The word *rechem* in both of these instances can be understood as a literal, physical womb or at least as the inability to bring forth a conception to be housed in the womb. Now let's see what else this word can show us.

Genesis 43 records the account of Joseph's brothers traveling to Egypt for food. When Joseph sees his brother, Benjamin, verse 30 states, "Joseph hurried out for *he was deeply stirred* (a form of *rachamim*) over his brother, and he sought a place to weep; and he entered his chamber and wept there." The words for "he was deeply stirred" literally read, "his womb grew warm." The brothers do not recognize Joseph, but he recognizes them. He is deeply stirred—his womb grew warm, his womb turned over, he had a tender feeling in his gut for his long-estranged brother—and he weeps.

These non-theological usages of *rechem* and *rachamim* show us how the words can be used both to describe a physical womb, as well as the gut-level, often gut-wrenching, feelings people experience for those they long for and love. The place where life is protected and nurtured, the physical womb, becomes the place from which the desire for protection and nurturing is birthed.

God's Compassion

We will turn now to passages where the word compassion is used to describe the character and behavior of God. Bear in mind the fact compassion carries the idea of tenderness for one who came from you, and that we are made in God's image. When thought of in conjunction with God's covenantal lovingkindness, the compassion of God is overwhelming in its depth and breadth. Consider how these theological usages of words for compassion grow your understanding of Who God is, as well as who He has made you to be as His image-bearer.

Hosea 1:6-7 states, "Then she conceived again and gave birth to a daughter. And the Lord said to [Hosea], 'Name her Lo-*ruhamah*, for I will no longer have *compassion* on the house of Israel, that I would ever forgive them. But I will have *compassion* on the house of Judah and deliver them…'" In Hebrew, the wordplay is evident as the child is named "Lo-ruhamah" ("Lo" means "no"; "ruhamah" is a form of *rachamim*) because the Lord is choosing to withhold His *rachamim* ("compassion") from Israel but extend His *rachamim* ("compassion") to Judah.

God is telling the Israelites because their rebellion has gone on so long, because of the covenant of His lovingkindness (Deuteronomy 28—blessing and cursing), He chooses to remove His compassion from them for a time. His grace, of course, will bring them back in a sense, and part of His covenant lovingkindness is the promise a remnant will always be protected. But in the general sense, He chooses to remove His compassion to allow the Israelites to experience discipline, which was promised if they did not walk according to the Law. God is removing His compassion for a time from those who did not have compassion on others as He had taught and instructed them to have.

The Lord also uses positive motivation to instruct His people. In Hosea 2:19 we read, "I will betroth you to Me forever; Yes, I will betroth you to Me in righteousness and in justice, in lovingkindness and in *compassion* (*rachamim*)." So many of these words are the notes of the biblical song—righteousness, justice, lovingkindness, and compassion. This works similarly to much of the music we love, in which common notes are arranged in such a way we enjoy and appreciate. God uses the notes of lovingkindness, compassion, justice, mercy, as the notes in His song. In this passage, God is describing Himself as a husband to the nation of Israel, and He is expressing to Israel what He is bringing to the table of their marriage. One of the qualities He brings is compassion, a deep love and tenderness from His "womb" for His people.

Psalm 51:1 says, "Be gracious to me, O God, according to Your lovingkindness; according to the greatness of your *compassion* (*rachamim*) blot out my transgressions." After his sin with Bathsheba is confronted, David appeals to God, asking Him to treat him not according to his actions, but according to God's covenantal love and tenderness toward David. His plea to God is, essentially, "However enduring your lovingkindness is, I want it. However tender your womb can be, I need it. Please be as gracious to me as You are kind and compassionate."

David is a wise man. He does not approach God as Job did, imploring Him for justice and ending up in a courtroom brawl with the Creator of the universe. Rather, David asks God for lovingkindness and compassion, for an undeserved display of mercy. David's sin with Bathsheba and his ill-treatment of Uriah were violations of the sixth and seventh commandments. David deserves wrath, but he asks for the opposite. He is so convinced of the possibility God might be compassionate that he asks Him to be so, and to give an equal measure of lovingkindness as well. He acknowledges what is deserved is death, and asks that God might, by way of His compassion, give David life, and God does.

If Psalm 103:13 has anything to say about it, fathers have "wombs" as well. The passage reads "just as a father has *compassion* (*rachamim*) on his children, so the Lord has *compassion* (*rachamim*) on those who fear Him." Like a dad who knows his children well, has seen them experience difficult times, and has stooped low to pick them up when they have fallen, so God relates to those who fear (some translations say "those who draw near to") Him.

As we saw in Lamentations 3:20-24, Jeremiah writes of many of God's attributes, three of which we have now studied together in this book. Personally devastated at the fall of Jerusalem by the hands of the Babylonians, the "weeping prophet" laments, "This I recall to mind, therefore I have hope. The Lord's lovingkindnesses (*hesed*) indeed never cease, for His compassions (*rachamim*) never fail. They are new every morning; great is Thy faithfulness (from *aman*). The Lord is my portion, says my soul, therefore I have hope in Him."

Again, take special note of Jeremiah's "formula" for dealing with tragedy. First, he determined to recall the character of God which he has already sealed in his mind. Then, he experienced the result of his recollection—hope. But it is the contemplation of the specific nature of each attribute of God's character as well as their powerful combination that produced the hope in Jeremiah's heart. And neatly arranged in the very center of the attributes he recalled was God's *rachamim,* the deep stirring of His womb for His people in the hour of their deepest need.

Did He Just Say "Bowels"?

For sixteen years I taught Bible and Theology at the College of Biblical Studies in Houston, Texas, where 60% of the student population was African American. Of the 60%, most grew up with the King James Version (KJV) of the Bible and regularly brought it to class. So, to be able to respond to the text they were typically reading, I familiarized myself with the KJV. It's possible many of you grew up with this version as well or it's more than likely your parents did, and almost certainly your grandparents did. For all of the confusing words and phrases to our modern ears, the King James translation of 1 John 3:17 paints a vivid, if not a bit disquieting, picture of compassion.

In the KJV, 1 John 3:17 reads "But whoso hath this

world's good, and seeth his brother have need, and shutteth up his *bowels of compassion* from him, how dwells the love of God in him?"

Yes, you read it correctly. *Splágchnon*, the Greek word for compassion, is translated here as "bowels of compassion" in the KJV which was written in 1611 when the "bowels" were considered the seat of all emotions. It's the area in which we feel compassion. Today, we might say, "My stomach (or gut) turned over when I saw that pitiful scene." So John, through the nuance of the King James translation, is stating that someone who is prompted by tender feelings of care for another but withholds aid is suffering from "compassion constipation." It sounds trite, or like an attempt at humor, but it is true to the text. Compassion is not meant to be "shutteth up" within us.

The Apostle Paul employed forms of *splágchnon* several times in his epistles. He exhorts his readers to see the great value of "compassion" as seen in these verses:

For God is my witness, how I long for you all with the *affection* of Christ Jesus. (Philippians 1:8).

Therefore if there is any encouragement in Christ, if there is any consolation of love, if there is any fellowship of the Spirit, if any *affection* and compassion. (Phil. 2:1).

So, as those who have been chosen of God, holy and beloved, put on a heart of *compassion*, kindness, humility, gentleness and patience. (Colossians 3:12).

For I have come to have much joy and comfort in your love, because the *hearts* of the saints have been refreshed through you, brother. (Philemon 7).

I have sent him back to you in person, that is, sending my very *heart*. (Philemon 12).

Yes, brother, let me benefit from you in the Lord; refresh my *heart* in Christ. (Philemon 20).

As we can see, the term describes one's capacity to express deep feelings and actions of true compassion ("affection" or "heart"). It is also important to note the powerful impact that well-expressed compassion can have on others. I love that Paul asks Philemon (one of the three recipients of the original letter) to "refresh my *heart* in Christ" in Philemon 20.

Philemon had refreshed the *hearts* of the saints (Philemon 7). Accordingly, Paul asked him to refresh his own *heart* by forgiving and accepting Onesimus. In each of these verses *splágchnon*, the New Testament equivalent of the Hebrew *rachamim*, is rendered "heart." Even the great Apostle Paul needed his own capacity for compassion to be re-energized and refreshed!

The Compassion of Christ

Of course, the best example of any of God's attributes is Jesus Christ. And so when it comes to the beautiful expression of compassion there are no more powerful biblical usages of *splágchnon* ("compassion") than those found in the Gospels. Let's take a look at three of these usages and see that Christ's *splágchnon* ("compassion") was often the powerful motivator behind His healings, His teaching, and His care for individuals.

Matthew 20:29-34 records the healing of two blind men who were sitting by the road outside of Jericho. Jesus and the great multitude that was following Him were making their way to Jerusalem for the upcoming Passover feast. The blind men, recognizing the greatness of Jesus, called out to Him twice, each time referred to Him as "Son of David" and each time asked Him for mercy. Jesus stopped and asked them what they wished for Him to do. Verses 33-34 state what happened next—"They said to Him, 'Lord, we want our eyes to be opened.' Moved with *compassion*, Jesus touched their eyes; and immediately they regained their sight and followed Him." Interestingly, the Greek text only uses the verbal form of *splágchnon* ("to have compassion").

The English words "moved with" are added by translation editors in an attempt to show the action true compassion produces. The Lord's inner reservoir of *splágchnon* immediately went to work as the text described His action—He touched their eyes. Sometimes things are so simple we might miss them. In this case, we see His compassion "moving out" toward someone else, the telltale sign of *splágchnon* (NT) and *rachamim* (OT).

Jesus' ministry of teaching was motivated by His capacity for compassion as well. Mark 6:30-34 provides an excellent example. The story reveals Jesus' desire to withdraw with his disciples to a lonely place and rest. His disciples were so busy attending to the needs of the multitude that the disciples had not eaten. The scene is almost comical as Jesus and His disciples got into a large boat, sailed to a lonely place for some rest, but were recognized by many in the large crowd who had run ahead and arrived before Jesus and the disciples.

I think it's in moments like this where we best see the heart of the Lord. Where we might be frustrated at this predicament, perhaps angry with the crowd that just won't leave us alone, Jesus responded differently. Drawing from His deep capacity for compassion, we see in 6:34, "When Jesus went ashore, He saw a large crowd, and He felt *compassion* for them because they were like sheep without a shepherd; and He began to teach them many things." Did you see it? The action that accompanied *compassion* in this instance was teaching! In fact, He taught them "many things," well in keeping with His deep well of compassion.

Jesus' personal, tender care of individuals has transformed the hearts and minds of people for 2,000 years. It's easy to imagine a God Who takes care of the "big stuff." After all, "He's got the whole world in His hands," right? Seems like that might take up most of His time, so certainly, we wouldn't expect God to express His compassion toward just one person, would we? But the song goes on to report that He's also got "you and me brother" and "you and me sister" as well as "the itty-bitty baby in His hands." Accordingly, the Lord's compassionate care for the individual is beautifully portrayed in His encounter with a widow as seen next.

Luke 7:11-17. Let's zoom in on the historical and cultural context in this account. The scene is tough to stomach. As is the case in the setting of many of Christ's miracles, extreme circumstances prevail. In this case, the situation is a funeral, the funeral of a young man, the only son of a widow. The common means of support no longer exist in this widow's life, especially in first-century Israelite culture. She's lost her husband and now her only son. How will she manage? Who will care for her on this difficult day and throughout her later years?

Providentially, as Jesus and His entourage are coming into her town, she and the funeral procession are heading out of town. Jesus surmises the overall scene but focuses His attention primarily on the widow as seen in verse 13, "When the Lord saw her, He felt *compassion* for her, and said to her, 'do not weep.'" But it was the action that proceeded from His compassion that halted the funeral procession on the spot as Jesus approached the coffin, grasped it, and commanded the dead son to "arise." Not only did the boy sit up, but also he began to speak. And then with these tender words at the end of verse 15, Luke records, "And Jesus gave him back to his mother."

Now that's a funeral! A funeral procession headed out of town is met by the Lord coming into town. A funeral shrouded with death is saturated with life. A young man is allowed to live and beautifully "given back to his mother" by Jesus. A widow is granted a future free from poverty and want. And at the center of all these life-giving blessings, we see the deep reservoir of Christ's compassion.

Wrapping Up

I mentioned earlier some think of compassion as synonymous with pity, with a feeling of sadness for someone's plight or the circumstances of a group of people. While compassion may include that feeling, it cannot end there. Compassion is a feeling that compels one toward action. It is not seeing a sad infomercial and flipping the channel.

Rather, compassion is seeing a person in need, just like the passage in 1 John 3 described, and *not* shutting off aid. Instead, it moves toward the person and their needs, seeking to meet them in accord with the depth of tender feelings their situation stirs up. This is not to say we only engage those in need when our feelings lead us to. Rather, we look to the character of God, to the One whose compassion is what keeps breath in our lungs, and seek to act in accord with His tenderness toward us. And when we do this, the feelings will often follow.

For further study:

2 Samuel 24:14	Isaiah 45:6	Matthew 14:14
1 Kings 3:26	Isaiah 49:13-15	Matthew 15:32
Neh. 9:9-31	Isaiah 64:15	Mark 1:41
Hosea 2:4	Matt 9:13, 36	Mark 8:2
Micah 7:18-19	Matthew 12:7	

CHAPTER 11

PEACE
Shalom | Eirēnē

I wish that I could say
The world was one and fighting was a fable
And the greed would turn the tables
I wish for peace, I wish for peace
I wish that I could see
A world that can be free with no more crying
Oh, but some of us are trying
I wish for peace, I wish for peace.
I Wish for Peace
Michelle Tumes

When peace like a river attendeth my way,
when sorrows like sea billows roll;
whatever my lot, thou hast taught me to say,
"It is well, it is well with my soul."
It Is Well
Horatio G. Spafford

The Lord bless you, and keep you;
The Lord make His face shine on you,
and be gracious to you;
The Lord lift up his countenance on you,
and give you peace.
Numbers 6:24-26

OUR NEXT WORD IS "PEACE," often depicted in Hebrew by the word *shalom* (from *shalem*) and in Greek by the word *eirēnē*, from which we get the English name "Irene." Peace may bring images of hippies to your mind, flower children posed in 1960's garb, index and middle fingers pointed upward. Perhaps you think of the absence of distracting or distressing sounds, reminiscent of the phrase, "peace and quiet," or the somber refrain "rest in peace" spoken when someone has died. You may imagine a world without war, a relationship without conflict, a vacation without work, or a "Peaceful Easy Feeling" as the Eagles so eloquently phrased.

While all of the ideas bring various bits of truth about peace to the table, what we see arising from a Scriptural understanding of peace is much richer. The Bible will show us peace is not merely the absence of strife, nor is it an esoteric ideal. Rather, it is an integral feature of God's character and design for our world, and the world to come.

Biblical peace carries with it the idea of something, or someone, or somewhere, being complete, whole, full, lacking in nothing. Peace paints the picture of a system wholly intact and functioning properly, with no loss of energy, no leaks. The system is set up well, and it is working well, like a water system that courses through a city such that the flowers at each individual's home are watered properly. The integrated system was built to fulfill a certain purpose, and it is doing so.

I Hadn't Thought of Peace Like This!

As we begin to consider some of the non-theological usages of the words for "peace" in Scripture, bear in mind the concept of a well-intentioned system working well. Genesis 15:15-16 reads, "And as for you, you shall go to your fathers in *peace*; you shall be buried at a good old age. Then the fourth generation they shall return here, for the iniquity of the Amorite is not yet *complete*." Both *shalom* and *shalem* are used here for "peace" and "complete," respectively. God is telling Abram that when he dies, he will be kept intact, protected—he will be at peace. He also states, "The iniquity of the Amorite is not yet *complete*," meaning that what is meant to find fullness ("inequity," in this case!) has yet not found it—*shalem* is still yet to occur.

You may recall from our study of the word "righteous" (*tsaddiq*) the portion of the Law that instructed the Israelites to deal with one another fairly in the marketplace. Remember the Norman Rockwell painting with the butcher weighing the scale down and the shopper lifting it up? We saw God's desire for a "just (righteous) weight" in Deuteronomy 25, juxtaposed with the self-seeking human nature on display in the Rockwell painting.

But there is another word God adds to His description of how transactions should occur. Deuteronomy 25:15 states, "You shall have a *full* and just weight; you shall have a *full* and just measure, that your days may be prolonged in the land which the Lord your God gives you." The word "full" is *shalem*. You shall have a weight and measure that are complete. If your weight is understood to weigh five pounds, it should weigh the full five pounds. You are to use weights and measures that are whole, functioning within the system as they are supposed to.

Though we do not commonly use the word "full" this way in modern vernacular, there are some examples of its usage in English. For example, in The Gettysburg Address, President Abraham Lincoln stated, "It is rather for us to be here dedicated to the great task remaining before us—that from these honored dead we take increased devotion to that cause for which they gave the last **full measure of devotion**—that we here highly resolve that these dead shall not have died in vain."[5] The men who died on the battlefield were, in Lincoln's estimation, those who had given of themselves a devotion that was whole, that was complete, that was full.

Popular expressions over the years have nicely captured this idea of "fullness" as well. Although their origin may be unclear, phrases like these have been used to describe situations where nothing was left out, where the "full" product was promised or delivered. Have you ever heard someone say, "the whole nine yards?" How about "the whole ball of wax?" The "whole enchilada" is classic. Let's not leave out "the whole shooting match, shebang or hog."

We are going to look at another passage in Deuteronomy now, for two reasons. The first is that it includes another use of *shalem*. The second is this—if you want to familiarize yourself with the SparkNotes version of the OT, study Deuteronomy. There is so much to be mined from Deuteronomy about the character of God and His intentions for His people. It may seem like one of "those boring law books" at first, but look for the claims about Who God is and His intricate plans for humanity. He is a holistic, specific, communicating God, and Deuteronomy displays that beautifully.

In Deuteronomy 27:6-7 we read, "You shall build the altar of the Lord your God of *uncut* stones; and you shall offer on it burnt offerings to the Lord your God; and you

---

[5] Lincoln, Abraham. "The Gettysburg Address." 1863. *America's Most Famous Speeches*, by Dale Salwak, Random House, 1984.

shall sacrifice *peace* offerings and eat there, and you shall rejoice before the Lord your God." Both "uncut" and "peace" are *shalem*, which I find to be very helpful in understanding the idea of *shalem* conceptually and as a word picture. The stones the Israelites used to build the altar were to be uncut—whole, intact. And, the offerings they made to God were to be offerings of wholeness and fullness as well. Peace offerings were the only offerings to be brought when enjoying peace with God. They serve, too, as the forbearer to the Lord's Supper, where we remember and celebrate the peace we have with God through the shed blood and risen body of Jesus Christ.

Psalm 38:3 states, "There is no soundness in my flesh because of Your indignation; there is no *health* in my bones because of my sin." While an individual's deliberate sin is certainly not the only reason he or she may become sick, the Scriptures indicate sin can cause a lack of wellness, or dis-ease. Sin interrupts everything that is whole and complete, keeping the fully integrated system of the body from working.

When we lie, we feel the heart rate rise and the face begins to flush. If we treat someone poorly, we will often use phrases like, "I've had a pit in my stomach ever since that interaction." Our bodies, while they surely break down because of the general fallenness of the world, respond also to our individual sin, because God created us to be physically, mentally, emotionally, and spiritually at peace. All parts of us are meant to be a fully functioning system, and when one part is not functioning well, the system is no longer intact. So, the psalmist here uses *shalom* for "health," indicating his body is not at peace, all is not well, because of his sin.

Perfect Peace

In Isaiah 26:3 we read, "The steadfast of mind You will keep in *perfect peace*, because he trusts in you." Perfect peace is literally *"shalom shalom"*—"peace peace." Remember how we learned that *rachamim,* the plural for "womb," conveyed the idea of a full feeling of tenderness for the one who comes from your womb? The double usage of "peace" here is similar to the way the plural expresses extra emphasis. Isaiah is stating those whose minds are stayed on the Lord will be kept in absolute, completely complete, wholly whole, fully full peace. They will, we might say, **for sure** be kept in peace. It's a certainty.

Numbers 6:24-26 states, "The Lord bless you, and keep you; the Lord make His face shine on you, and be gracious to you; the Lord lift up his countenance on you, and give you *peace (shalom)*." This is known as the Aaronic Blessing, which God instructed Moses to speak over Aaron and his sons. God's desire for His people as seen throughout all of Scripture, and specifically in this passage, is they may have perfect peace in relationship with Him. He desires their hands, minds, and hearts to be connected, a whole system intact, working effectively to the glory of God and good of others, just as God intended at creation.

Wholly Devoted

Solomon is a biblical character who typically evokes strong reactions in those who know his story. Most often, Solomon is remembered for his poor finish in life. Seduced by his many foreign wives and their false gods, Solomon's heart was turned away from the Lord. After Solomon's death, the united kingdom of Israel was divided and weakened. But Solomon's beginning was another story. In one of the hidden gems of the Bible, 1 Kings 8, we see a different Solomon, a king in love with the Lord, a king leading his people toward the things of God, a king dedicating the temple in Jerusalem to the service and worship of God.

At the end of Solomon's words to the people of Israel, we read in 1 Kings 8:61, "Let your heart therefore be *wholly devoted* to the Lord our God, to walk in His statutes and to keep His commandments, as at this day." The two-word English phrase "wholly devoted" translates the single term *shalem* in this verse, beautifully depicting *shalem's* concept of fullness, of wholeness. Certainly, the idea that our hearts should be fully devoted **to** the Lord is valid. The direction, if you will, of our full devotion should be **towards** the Lord. He should always be the very center of our attention, the One around Whom our lives are arranged.

However, there's another way to look at this verse that may reveal a different layer of the idea of "whole/full devotion." The term translated "to" is the Hebrew *'im,* which is most often rendered as the preposition "with" or "in." This term conveys the notion of commonality, of togetherness. In fact, in 1 Kings 8 alone, there are ten usages of *'im.* Except for 8:61, the term is translated "with" or "in," emphasizing the ideas of commonality and togetherness. However, the same Hebrew term (*'im*) is translated "to" only in 8:61, thus raising the question why wouldn't the term be translated "with" or "in" as seen elsewhere throughout the passage?

Instead of, "Let your heart therefore be *wholly devoted* **to** the Lord," perhaps a more precise understanding could be, "Let your heart therefore be full or complete **with** the Lord." What a powerful image this reveals. What if Solomon's blessing of the people was that at the core of their being (the heart), they would be full or complete **with** God? In other words, "Let your heart therefore be complete with God, at peace with Him." That which humanity lacks is sourced and supplied through God, received by being complete only with Him, therefore at "peace" with Him. Let us be wholly devoted to the Lord!

New Testament Examples of Peace

Let's turn now to a few instances of *eirēnē*, the Greek word for "peace," in the New Testament.

Romans 5:1 states, "Therefore, having been justified by faith, we have *peace (eirēnē)* with God through our Lord Jesus Christ." Peace is so rich with meaning here. To be at peace with God, justified by faith, means we are no longer enemies of God. We are no longer at war with him, our purposes and postures at odds. Rather, we have been united in Jesus, rendered allies with one another. However, the imagery does not stop at just a ceasefire between humanity and God. It is not merely that conflict has been quieted, but that in Jesus, we are reunited with God. It is as if we are the hose and God is the water supply, and through Jesus Christ, we become reconnected to the water system, as we were always meant to be.

Even after sin invaded the human race in Genesis 3, people maintained the capacity to be united back to God, to be joined with Him through the instrument of faith. Belief in the Lord Jesus Christ links us back to the source so we can do what we were intended to do—be vessels of His supply. When we are at peace with God through salvation made possible by the death and resurrection of His Son, Jesus Christ, we can be who we were intended to be.

Lastly, consider Philippians 4:6-7, which states, "Be anxious for nothing, but in everything by prayer and supplication with thanksgiving let your requests be made known to God. And the *peace* (*eirēnē*) of God which transcends all understanding will guard your hearts and minds in Christ Jesus." Notice the similarity to lovingkindness. The feeling of tenderness often follows the decision to love loyally, to show lovingkindness. Here in Philippians 4, the emotional experience of the peace of God results from the fact that He hears our prayers and supplications, willing, desirous that we come to Him with our requests.

Interestingly, the phrase "the peace of God" is found only here in the New Testament but it provides a powerful image to consider. The result of praying about our concerns and requests will yield for us (in some measure) God's own peace, His wholeness, His completeness, His full guard around our inner being. Prayer allows us to enter into the fullness of God's very presence, and we are different because of the encounter.

More Than a Feeling

Peace is more than a feeling, but not less than a feeling. It is more than a system, but not less than a system. Peace is wholeness, completion, the fullness of reality as it is meant to be, the awareness that things are sound. Of course, we will not experience absolute fullness of peace until Jesus returns, releasing us forever from the presence of sin and its constant effect on our lives. But we see glimpses of it now—in the pursuit of human flourishing, in the moment of Communion, in a treasured relationship. And someday, those glimpses of wholeness and surety will become all there is to see.

"Blessed are the peacemakers, for they shall be called sons of God." (Matthew 5:9).

For further study:

Leviticus 3:1	1 Kings 15:14
Joshua 8:31 (2x)	1 Chronicles 29:19
1 Samuel 17:22	Amos 1:6, 9
1 Samuel 25:5	Matthew 10:13
1 Kings 6:7	

CHAPTER 12

PRAISE
Halal | Epainos

Morning has broken like the first morning
Blackbird has spoken like the first bird
Praise for the singing
Praise for the morning
Praise for them springing fresh from the world.
Morning Has Broken
Eleanor Farjeon

Praise to the Lord, the Almighty, the King of creation!
O my soul, praise Him, for He is thy health and salvation!
All ye who hear, now to His temple draw near;
Praise Him in glad adoration.
Praise to the Lord, the Almighty
Joachim Neander

Praise the Lord!
Praise, O servants of the Lord,
Praise the name of the Lord.
Blessed be the name of the Lord
From this time forth and forever.
From the rising of the sun to its setting
The name of the Lord is to be praised.
Psalm 113:1-3

WE HAVE REACHED OUR LAST KEY WORD, our final attempt at unlocking a bit of text within the Scriptures that may help you understand the Bible all the more. "Halal," the Hebrew word for "praise" will become the crescendo to our time together.

In the first five chapters, we uncovered the story of our relationship with God. Seen first in its perfection and wholeness through the word *ezer* (helper), the world was quickly torn apart by *chata* (sin). God provides a mechanism for us to be united with him through *aman* (faith) in Him, which renders us *tsaddiq* (righteous) in His sight. We often refer to this as "getting saved" or *yasha* (salvation). These words paint a picture for us of how God created the world to be, how Adam and Eve's sin caused it to fall, and how God made a way for us to be brought back into communion with Him.

The next six words told of the characteristics of God, which not only comprise who He is, but how He created the world and how it should function. We discovered the richness of God's grace (*chen*), the key distinctive of biblical Christianity. He extends it to us as an absolutely free gift, no strings, uncaused, unearned, just received. We learned when God is to be given glory (*kabod*) it doesn't simply mean we should think of Him with lights flashing all around and angels bowing down to Him. Rather, we should recognize He is a God Who must be dealt with, He is important, and the way we live our lives a reflection of our reaction to His importance. We saw God as holy (*qodesh*), set apart, "wholly other" in His being and essence. We were enriched by His *hesed*, His covenantal-binding lovingkindness, as well as His *rachamim*, a deep tenderness propelling Him to action for us, and His *shalom*, the fact that He is complete in and of Himself and desires wholeness in our lives. Each of these characteristics convinces us a bit more that God really is as good as He says He is.

A firmer grasp of each of these characteristics should strengthen our faith a bit more, convincing us the story of God as seen in the Bible is, in fact, true. For, if there is a God who is this gracious, this glorious, this holy, this full of lovingkindness, compassion, and peace, then that is exactly the kind of God Who would make a way for us to be near to Him forever.

It's Time to Respond with Reasons to Praise!

So now, in response to this great God Who has paved the way for our ultimate salvation, we turn to the words in Scripture for "praise." The Hebrew word is *halal*, as seen in "*hallel*-ujah." the Greek word is *epainos.* At the core of each of these words is something of such great importance that we will continually revisit it throughout this chapter—*halal* and *epainos* only make sense if they are being used to praise someone or something **for a reason.** As we consider various examples of praise in Scripture, and even share some instances of modern occurrences where we offer praise, I think this will crystallize for us.

To praise is to commend for a **reason**. Praising is the deep inner acknowledgment and outward expression of superiority or greatness, resulting in the citation of specific **reasons** or examples regarding what or who is being considered superior or great. This is similar to the ideas of "glory" and "holy," where we saw it only makes sense to respond to God in view of His importance and distinct nature.

To praise is to exalt or lift up another. More colloquially, it's the general concept of "bragging on" somebody. And, of course, when we brag on somebody, we don't just say, "I'm bragging on my friend John!" and leave it at that, right? Rather, we say, "I am so proud of my friend, John! He led our team with excellence today." We know and state the reasons for our praise; otherwise, the praise is empty at best, nonsensical at worst.

Perhaps one of the best illustrations of this is how men often behave at a football game. I talk regularly with men who say they do not have a wide range of emotions and have trouble expressing praise, especially when it comes to God. But if I attend a football game with them at Kyle Field (where the Texas A&M Aggies play), suddenly our emotions and expressions are on full display.

They do not glance casually over at me, commenting softly that a play was well executed or whisper they were pleased to see the accumulation of six points as a result of a touchdown. Rather, they jump up and down, ecstatic, hands waving in the air as they shout, "DID YOU SEE THAT PLAY? Our quarterback is amazing! What a throw! Man, he threaded the needle on that one!" In the presence of what they deem to be praiseworthy, emotional and descriptive responses flow from their lips. They are praising—making observations and then speaking of them.

Again, praise is the deep inner acknowledgment and outward expression of superiority or greatness. The person who is praising is responding to something he or she finds to be special, to be worthy of praise. We should commend, we should praise—for a reason—and we should state the reason! Keep this in mind as we begin to read passages of Scripture that use the words for praise. What are the **reasons** that praise is being offered? What makes something or someone worthy of praise, and how is that praise to be expressed?

These Things are Praiseworthy...Really?

In Genesis 12:14-15 we read, "It came about when Abram came into Egypt, the Egyptians saw that the woman [Sarai] was very beautiful. Pharaoh's officials saw her and *praised* (*halal*) her to Pharaoh; and the woman was taken into Pharaoh's house." Pharaoh's officials quite simply, are praising Sarai's physical beauty to Pharaoh. They are not commenting on her spiritual state, nor anything related to her character, which shows us that "praise" in the Bible can be non-theological, just like the other words we have encountered. People in Scripture are not always praising God, or even godly characteristics in one another. Sometimes, they are just seeing something or someone beautiful, and they talk about it, which is the essence of what it is to praise.

Similarly, 2 Samuel 14:25 states, "Now in all Israel was no one as handsome as Absalom, so highly *praised* (*halal*); from the sole of his foot to the crown of his head there was no defect in him." Absalom, similarly to Sarai, was praised for his physical attractiveness. According to the text, he was flawless in appearance, and people liked to talk about it. This is, again, the essence of praise— something is observed in a person or thing that warrants acknowledgment, and that acknowledgment finds its fulfillment in specifically extolling the merits of the person or thing through words.

So far we've seen praise for Sarai's beauty and Absalom's handsomeness. Both of the examples reveal "praise" is not reserved just for God in the Bible. To seal the deal of this point, consider the praise given in Judges 16:24, "When the people saw him, they *praised* their god, for they said, 'Our god has given our enemy into our hands, even the destroyer of our country, who has slain many of us.'"

What we have here in Judges 16 is a beautiful example of non-theological usage of a word. It's non-theological in the sense it's not involving the God of the Bible. The Philistines are praising their god, Dagon, because they perceive him to be the one who has delivered them from their enemies. They are wrong in their estimation, of course, and that very night Samson toppled the pillars holding up the house, bringing to an end those who had just been celebrating their victory through praise of a false god.

Nevertheless, the word *halal* is the word used here, not because Scripture is saying Dagon is actually worthy of praise, but because the Philistines' "praise" was genuine to them, it was real to them. It also offers us an insightful glimpse into the real usage and meaning of biblical *halal*, specifically the deep acknowledgment and expression of superiority or greatness, regardless of the object of the praise.

In Proverbs 31:30-31 we read, "Charm is deceitful and beauty is vain, but a woman who fears the Lord, she shall be *praised* (*halal*). Give her the product of her hands, and let her works *praise* (*halal*) her in the gates."

We see a fuller description of this woman in the preceding section (31:10-29). The "Proverbs 31 Woman" is to be praised for a variety of reasons—for the excellent wife she is to her husband, her highly skilled work, her tender care for others, her relationship with her children, and her deep respect for God. In 31:31 her "works" are praised specifically.

All that the woman has made with her hands, the fruits of her labor, that which she has produced for the good of her family and community, is now extolled by others. This provides a noteworthy biblical example of what it is to be thought of and spoken of as praiseworthy.

When someone does an excellent job, let us say it to that person as well as others! List the reasons!

In regards to the Proverbs 31 Woman, let us make a few points. The goal of Proverbs is to impart wisdom into the hearts, minds, and hands of its readers. Throughout the book, the value and virtue of wisdom is lifted up for all to consider and embrace. The Hebrew root verb for wisdom is *hakam* (or *chakam*) and the term is most often expressed as a feminine noun (*hokmah* or *chokmah*), and conveys the idea of "skill," often in contexts where "skillful living" is discussed.

Knowledge is understanding **what** to do. Wisdom knows both **what** to do and **how** to do it. Consider all the products in the world that require skill to make. How about the laptops Abby and I are using to type the words of this book? Can you make one from scratch without a pretty high level of skill? I can't. How about this chair I'm sitting in? Above my skill level. This table? Nope, I don't have the skill. Accordingly, the Book of Proverbs offers the "skill" to live life well in an unwavering manner—chapter after chapter, verse upon verse.

And so it makes sense that in the final chapter, we see the heroine of the entire book, *hokmah* (the feminine noun for "wisdom"), personified in the character and actions of the "Proverbs 31 Woman," who serves as the beautiful finale to the Book of Proverbs. The finale allows us to see she actually serves two purposes—1) a wise and skillful wife to seek to imitate (respectful of God, industrious in her work, loving her family well) and 2) a closing symbol of skillful living for all (men and women alike) to seek to imitate.

Praise in the Psalms

Psalms 113-118 form what is known as the *Hallel,* the Hymns of Praise, which were to be sung at the Festivals of Passover, Pentecost, and Tabernacles, as well as the Festival of the Dedication and New Moons. As a domestic celebration of the Passover, Psalms 113 and 114 would be sung before the meal, and Psalms 115-118 after it, when the fourth cup had been filled. Psalm 118, at least, was probably a hymn sung by Jesus and His disciples in the upper room at their final Passover supper (Matthew 26:30). These psalms are filled with exclamations of praise for God for a whole host of reasons. Psalm 117 is a beautiful Hymn of Praise:

> "*Praise* the Lord, all nations;
> Laud Him, all peoples!
> For His lovingkindness is great toward us,
> And the truth of the Lord is everlasting.
> *Praise* the Lord!"

The psalmist calls the people to praise and **gives them reasons** to do so. His lovingkindness (*hesed*) is great! His truth (from *aman*) is everlasting! For these reasons then, we praise Him. In response to these wonderful realities of Who God is, may we acknowledge them and speak of them.

Psalms 146-150 are similar to the *Hallel* as they too are a praise-fest of Yahweh. These psalms are full of specific actions of the Lord the psalmist finds praiseworthy. For example, in Psalm 146:8-10 he writes,

> "The Lord opens the eyes of the blind;
> The Lord raises up those who are bowed down;
> The Lord loves the righteous;

The Lord protects the strangers;
He supports the fatherless and the widow,
But He thwarts the way of the wicked.
The Lord will reign forever,
Your God, O Zion, to all generations.
Praise the Lord."

In naming reason after reason why God is worthy of praise, the psalmist is making a case for the goodness of God, and then responding to his case in the only way that makes sense—a strong word for those who stand against this good God.

The Symphony of Ephesians 1 and Philippians 1

If these key biblical words are the notes of the song of Scripture, then Ephesians 1 is a symphony. In just one verse (1:6) we read God predestined his children, "…to the *praise* (*epainos*) of the *glory* of His *grace*, which He freely bestowed on us in the Beloved."

In other words, we see that the ultimate purpose of God as He calls us to Himself is for us to extol (praise) His "glorious grace." In this classic Pauline phrase, he reminds us of the importance/heaviness (*glory*) of the undeserved *grace* of God freely bestowed upon us. In other words, His grace is glorious!; His grace is a really big deal! Such important grace should elicit a response of praise. There is for us no greater reason to praise God—He has made a way for us to be united with Him, and it only makes sense we would speak of how wonderful this truth is to ourselves, to Him, to others.

Philippians 1:10-11 works similarly, stating, "So that you may approve the things that are excellent, in order to be sincere and blameless until the day of Christ; having been filled with the fruit of righteousness which comes through Jesus Christ, to the glory and *praise* (*epainos*) of God." Yet again, what do we see? Reasons! God's people approving excellence, being sincere and blameless, and being filled with the fruit of righteousness—these are realities that exist in response to Who God is; they are offerings of praise.

Breaking Down Hallelujah

If you happen to be a writer, a songwriter, or just someone who says "hallelujah" sometimes—consider carefully what you say before and after this word! Hallelujah means, "All of you, praise Yah(weh)!" The term is derived from the combination of:

Halal - the common Hebrew verb for praise
U - a symbol in Hebrew to indicate a plural command
Jah - an "English-ized" attempt to translate the shortened form of *Yah*weh

So, we see that (technically) the combination of these subcomponents produces the term, "Hallel-u-Yah," a COMMAND to go and praise God. The mere expression of "hallelujah" is not praise in and of itself. It is rather a command, an exhortation, an invitation for all of us to extol the Lord by citing specific attributes and actions of Yah(weh) as seen in the Bible or creation. So, let's beware of participating in the ridiculous scenario where everyone is running around saying, "Praise the Lord," but (sadly) no one is really praising the Lord!

If we are going to praise Yahweh well and fully, we need to say things about Him. We need to articulate the particulars. Note that up to the final chapter of the Psalter, this call to "articulate the particulars" is maintained, "Praise Him **for** His mighty deeds; praise

Him **according to** His excellent greatness." (Psalm 150:2). No wonder the Book of Psalms ends with such a lofty exhortation, "Let everything that has breath *praise* the Lord. *Praise* the Lord (*Halle*/ujah)!"

C.S. Lewis' discussion[6] on how praise is "natural" is beautifully explained here: "In any area of life one naturally praises what one appreciates—in fact, the praise is part of the enjoyment. To enjoy something fully one must speak of it. To praise God, then, means that people are enjoying His benefits. And when God calls people to praise Him, He is calling them to enjoy His benefits, so that they will have cause to praise."[7]

My Little "Yah" Rant

One of my (Buck's) pet peeves is how the name of Yahweh (or Yah) has been seemingly hidden in our English Bibles. First of all, there's the consistent use of "hallelujah" throughout modern English Bibles. When the Hebrew Bible was first translated into the King James Bible (KJV), all consonantal instances of *yod*, the first Hebrew letter in "Yah," were rendered with a *j*. With all due respect to the KJV and its editors, the shortened form of Yahweh's name is Yah, not Jah. It was an odd choice by the KJV as there is no "j" letter in Hebrew. And ironically, when we pronounce the term "hallelu*j*ah" we say "hallelu*y*ah," clearly using the "ya" sound as in *yank* or *yarn* or *yard*. We don't say "hallelu - "ja" as in *jazz*, *jab*, or *Jack*. So why not just transliterate the word correctly, go with "halleluyah" and thus preserve "Yah," the shortened form of Yahweh?

---

[6] C.S. Lewis, Reflections in the Psalms (New York: Harcourt, Brace and World, 1958). 90-98.

[7] Ross, Allen P. A Commentary of the Psalms: Volume 1 (1-41). Grand Rapids: Kregel Publications, 2011. Print. 120-121.

Secondly, I'm concerned we may be missing the fact that the Hebrew term "Yah" is included in many of the names found in the Bible, but the "Y" has been left off in English Bibles, producing a rather hollow and misleading "ah." Here's a list:

Nehemi*ah* - "comfort of Yah"
Isai*ah* - "salvation of Yah"
Jeremi*ah* - "exaltation of Yah"
Obadi*ah* - "servant of Yah"
Mic*ah* - "who is like Yah?"
Zephani*ah* - "Yah has concealed"
Zechari*ah* - "Yah has remembered"

The names above include "Yah" at the end. Here's a list of names that begin with the Hebrew "Yah." However (and utterly maddening), each name begins with the letter "J" in English Bibles and thus completely disguises the original inclusion of "Yah":

*J*oshua - "whose salvation is Yah"
*Je*hoshaphat - "whom Yah judges"
*J*onathan - "whom Yah gave"
*Je*hoiachin - "whom Yah has established"
*Je*horam - "Yah is exalted"

Lastly, what's up with "alleluia"? I realize it's the old Latin form of "hallelujah," but as time marches on "alleluia" (I fear) will become an unrecognizable form of "hallelujah." Alleluia drops the first letter of "hallelujah," somewhat understandable as the "ha" sound can be close to some expressions of "a" in English. The middle part of the alleluia is on point but the word crashes pretty hard at the end, right? "Yah" gets reduced to "ia," which for me is the single greatest contributing factor to my pet peeve. Some English words end in "ia," but we typically pronounce each of those two letters separately as in *claustrophobia* and *schizophrenia*. In fairness, we do have English words that vocalize the "ia" combo with a "ya" sound as in *pneumonia* and *nostalgia*. In any case, we've got to do something about getting the word out that "alleluia" is the same word as "hallelujah," which really should be rendered "halleluyah"!

Ok, I feel better now.

Our study of key biblical words has shown us a great deal about God that now warrants our response. *Praise* now gives us the key reaction word to that which we have now learned about God.

Because You created the world in perfect completion and will restore it in the world to come, because You sent Your Son to pay the penalty for our sin, because You provide access to You by faith, praise Your name!

Because You render us righteous in Your sight by faith, because Your salvation is so great, because You bestow upon us abundant grace, for your glory, praise Your name!

Because You are holy, because Your lovingkindness endures forever, because You move toward us in compassion, because You are the author and deliverer of peace, praise Your name!

Anyway, thanks for hanging with us. We hope this journey has been a blessing for you. It truly was for us.

All Thy works shall praise Thy name in earth and sky and sea...

For further study:

Ezekiel 26:11-17	Proverbs 28:4
Psalm 22:19-23	Jeremiah 20:13

ABOUT THE AUTHORS

Robert G. "Buck" Anderson, Jr. is a graduate of Dallas Theological Seminary (ThM, Old Testament Literature and Hebrew Exegesis, 1989) and the University of Houston (EdD, Higher Education Administration, 2001). Buck was a faculty member at College of Biblical Studies (CBS) in Houston, Texas from 1990-2006 as well as Academic Dean at CBS from 1993-2006. Since 2006, Buck has served as a pastor at Grace Bible Church in College Station, Texas, focusing on the areas of Leadership Development and Operations. Buck and his wife Val enjoy their wonderful family, including three daughters, two sons-in-law, and a bunch of grandkids. Find Buck here:

buckanderson52@gmail.com
buckanderson.com
@UnlockingKBW

Abby Anderson Perry is a freelance writer featured in publications such as *Christianity Today*, *Sojourners*, *The Gospel Coalition*, *Fathom Mag*, and *Christ and Pop Culture*. Abby holds a Masters of Biblical and Theological Studies from Dallas Theological Seminary. She lives with her husband and their two sons in Texas. Find her at abbyjperry.com and on Twitter @abbyjperry.

UNLOCKING KEY BIBLICAL WORDS CHEAT SHEET

English	**Helper**	**Sin**	**Faith**	**Righteous**
Hebrew	*ezer* *'ezer*	*chata* *chata'* *hata'*	*aman* *'aman*	*tsaddiq*
Greek	NA	*hamartanō*	*pisteuō*	*dikaiosynē*
Key Verses	Gen. 2:18 Gen. 2:20 Ex. 18:4	Jud. 20:16 Rom. 3:23	2 Kgs. 18:16 Gen. 15:6 Jn. 3:16	Dt. 25:13-15 Phil. 3:9
Concept	Complete Shield Protect Deliver Keep	Miss Fail to meet a standard Not right	Recognize strength or ability Consider as dependable	Meet (or satisfy) a standard
Keys to Unlock	Who is the helper? What kind of help?	Missed what standard? Variety of standards	Faith in what/who? Object not always God	Meet what standard? Variety of standards

UNLOCKING KEY BIBLICAL WORDS CHEAT SHEET

English	Save	Grace	Glory	Holy
Hebrew	yasha yasha'	chen hen	kabed kabod	qodesh
Greek	sōzō	cháris	dóxa	hágios
Key Verses	Ps. 12:1, 5 Ps. 25:5 Acts 4:12	Job 1:9; 2:3 2 Sam. 12:22 Eph. 2:8-9	1 Sam. 4:18 2 Sam. 14:26 Ezek. 21:21 Eph. 1:6-14	Genesis 38:20-22 1 Pet. 1:16
Concept	Deliver Rescue	Without cause Undeserved Unearned Absolutely Free	Literal: weighty, heavy Figurative: important	Set apart Not common Distinct Special
Keys to Unlock	Saved from what? Physical or spiritual?	Strings attached? Who knows?	Literal or Figurative? Who/what is heavy? Why?	Special prostitute Does NOT mean sinless

UNLOCKING KEY BIBLICAL WORDS CHEAT SHEET

English	Loving-kindness	Compassion	Peace	Praise
Hebrew	*hesed* *chesed*	*rachamim* *rechem*	*shalom* *shalem*	*halal*
Greek	NA	*splágchnon*	*eirēnē*	*epainos*
Key Verses	1 Samuel 20:12-17	Gen. 29:31 Hosea 1:6-7 1 John 3:17 Matt. 20:34	Genesis 15:15-16 1 Kgs. 8:61 Rom. 5:1 Phil. 4:6-7	Genesis 12:15 Ps. 150:6 Eph. 1:6, 12, 14
Concept	Loyalty to a deal or covenant Determined faithfulness	"Womb" love Tender feeling	Complete Whole Full Integral	Inner & outer express-ion of greatness
Keys to Unlock	"Glue" of relation-ship NT = faithfulness	Literal: womb Figure: full expression and action of the womb KJV = bowels	What or who is described as peace? Not always God	What / who is being praised? Reasons? Not always God

HOW TO DO A WORD STUDY

- The "key" to understanding word studies is to remember this little maxim: **the meaning of a word is determined by how it is used**. So, we are going to find out where a key word shows up in Scripture and spend some time with it, conduct an interview to see how it is **used**, discover what (or whom) it really is. Some interviews may feel a bit bland, but every once in a while, a few will be profound, helping us create a robust definition and understanding of the word.

- Get an Exhaustive Concordance that corresponds to your study Bible. For me, NASB (1995 update) and ESV are great. The NIV concordance is vastly improved but the verbiage in the NIV sometimes makes it difficult to find the original word(s). Strong's and NKJV are fine as well. Your results can vary slightly if you use an older version, but it's easy to work around it.

- The goal is to determine the original language word that was used before it was translated into your English Bible. **We want to do a word study on the original word!**

- Let's say you're reading through Genesis and come to 3:1 and see, "Now the serpent was more crafty than any beast of the field...." You're intrigued with the term "crafty" (good call!) and now you want to do a word study on the Hebrew term that is translated "crafty."

- Two ways to go now—Old School or New School. We'll look at both but please read the Old School approach first as it contains details helpful to both approaches.

- **Old School**: using an actual book known as a concordance (gasp!). Yes, this really works and still the primary method I use.

- So, now you're going to look up "crafty" in your concordance. Fortunately, your concordance of choice arranges all the English words found in your Bible in alphabetical order!

- You get to "crafty" in your concordance and then see the key part of the verse that intrigued you originally ("Now the serpent..."). Then, look to the right and you will see "Gen. 3:1" and to the right of that you will see "6175." That's our word! We're going to do a word study on "6175" (which is just a label assigned to that particular Hebrew term by a guy named James Strong in 1890).

- Now go to the back of your concordance, just after the alphabetical arrangement ends. This final section of your concordance contains all of Mr. Strong's numbers in (you guessed it!) numeric order. First, you will see a section just containing numbers that correspond to Hebrew terms (OT), then a subsequent section containing numbers that correspond to Greek terms (NT).

- So, we go to the Hebrew section because our verse (Gen. 3:1) is in the OT and we see 6175's entry as such: עָרוּם *arum* [791a]: from 6191: crafty, shrewd, sensible:—crafty 2, prudent 2, prudent man 3, sensible 2, sensible man 1, shrewd 1

- This is great information and all we need for an Old School word study. So, what do we do next?

- For basic studies like this, we're only going to study the Hebrew term "arum" (6175) and see that it has a general meaning of crafty, shrewd, sensible. More advanced word studies would also look at 6191 (*arom*), as 6175 is a part of the 6191 word family.

- Sticking with our 6175 plan, we now turn our attention to the next set of information: crafty 2, prudent 2, prudent man 3, sensible 2, sensible man 1, shrewd 1

- This means that 6175 (*arum*) is translated in the NASB (the Bible I'm using) as crafty 2 times, prudent/prudent man 5 times, sensible/sensible man 3 times, and shrewd 1 time. So, we just need to look at 11 OT verses that contain our word *arum* (6175) and we'll make great strides toward a fuller understanding of the word.

- We'll start with "crafty" and go back to the alphabetical section of your concordance and the same place where we first began our search. You'll see that "crafty" has 6175 to its right exactly 2 times—Gen. 3:1 and Job 15:5

- Now we're going to look up "prudent/prudent man" and find the 5 times that 6175 is translated "prudent/prudent man." They are all found in just 4 different chapters in Proverbs (a major clue to the meaning of the term). Here they are: Proverbs 12:16, 12:23, 13:16, 22:3, and 27:12.

- Now we're going to look up "sensible/sensible man" and find the 3 times that 6175 is translated "sensible/sensible man." They are all found in the same chapter in Proverbs (a major clue to the meaning of the term). Here they are: Proverbs 14:8, 14:15, and 14:18.

- Now onto our final clue, the 1 time that 6175 is

155

translated "shrewd" in the NASB—Job 5:12

- Now the fun part. Word studies combine science and art. We used the science part to discover our 11 clues. But now we need to employ some language arts skills to unlock the concept(s) that binds the 11 altogether. **After all, we're looking closely at a word family**. They have common themes and concepts just waiting to be discovered!

- Here's the lineup of the 11 verses:

Genesis 3:1	Prov. 13:16	Prov. 22:3
Job 15:5	Prov. 14:8	Prov. 27:12
Prov. 12:16	Prov. 14:15	Job 5:12
Prov. 12:23	Prov. 14:18	

- Let's show the "New School" approach next and then we can use the language arts skills on the results of both approaches at the end of this section.

- **New School**: using a Bible study web site that gets you to the original word and Strong's number faster ("the Science") but the same thorough analysis is required on "the Art" side.

- Go to: www.biblestudytools.com and create a free account.

- In the Search Bar in the middle of the screen, select "The Bible" (as this is what you want to search) and then type: Genesis 3:1. This is the verse that contains "crafty," the word we want to study. Now click "Find It" (to the right).

- Look just under the Search Bar and find **GENESIS 3:1** (in bold caps).

- To the right of **GENESIS 3:1** is a drop-down menu containing different versions of the Bible.

For this exercise, scroll down and click on "New American Standard Bible."

- The verse will appear below. Wait a second for the key words to turn blue (hyperlink). Now click on the word "crafty" within the verse and voilà!

- You should now see the same information us Old Schoolers discovered a different way:

- 6175 *arum* [791a]: from 6191: crafty, shrewd, sensible:—crafty 2, prudent 2, prudent man 3, sensible 2, sensible man 1, shrewd 1.

- Look at the upper right of the screen and you will see:
  - o   Genesis 1
  - o   Job 2
  - o   Proverbs 8

- Click on each of these 3 books to find the 11 verses in which *arum* (6175) occurs in the OT.

- **Word Study Worksheet**: Now you're ready to start a word study worksheet. On the worksheet, you should list and study EVERY passage that contains the word in which you are interested. Then ask basic types of investigatory kinds of questions of each passage: Who? What? When? Why? Where? How? etc.

- Your goal is to "unlock" the common concept(s) that all the verses convey. Listen to their stories. Find the common thread. We're looking closely at **a word family**. They have common themes, concepts, and stories. Let's go find them!

- See my analysis of *arum* as well as the blank word study worksheets on the following pages.

WORD STUDY ANALYSIS

Key Word: *arum* (6175): crafty, shrewd, sensible:—crafty 2, prudent 2, prudent man 3, sensible 2, sensible man 1, shrewd 1.

Analysis: *arum* (6175) is first used to describe the serpent in Genesis 3:1. Obviously but importantly, at that point in the story of Genesis, we don't know much about the serpent. We learn a few verses later that his goal was to tempt Adam and Eve into rebellion against God's clear command, viz., "But from the tree of knowledge of good and evil you shall not eat..." (Genesis 2:17a). We don't officially learn that the serpent is "the devil and Satan" until Revelation 12:9, although we had every right to be suspicious long before the final book of the Bible!

When it comes to word studies, and particularly our word (*arum*/6175), we need to be careful not to move too quickly to judgment regarding the "goodness or badness" of a term. Words are mere symbols for a concept; they have no intrinsic morality. So, with that in mind, and after an analysis of the other 10 times *arum* appears in the Hebrew OT, the evidence reveals that **arum is the skill of being aware, of garnering knowledge, of acting with knowledge, of being able to wisely identify an opponent, of being strategic with one's thoughts and actions**. That's why words like crafty, prudent, sensible and shrewd are used to describe this concept. As a result, the same skill can be used by a scheming enemy of God or the prudent seeking wisdom for God. The term (according to Eliphaz in Job 5:12) can even imply God's mighty *arum*: "He frustrates the plotting of the *shrewd* (*arum*), so that their hands cannot obtain success."

SAMPLE WORD STUDY WORKSHEET

Qs\VERSES				
WHO				
WHAT				
WHEN				
WHY				
WHERE				
HOW				
CONTEXT				
COMMENT				

SAMPLE WORD STUDY WORKSHEET

Qs\VERSES				
WHO				
WHAT				
WHEN				
WHY				
WHERE				
HOW				
CONTEXT				
COMMENT				

SHARE THE GOOD NEWS!

For God so loved the world, that He gave His only begotten Son, that whoever believes in Him shall not perish, but have eternal life. (John 3:16).

Now I make known to you, brethren, the gospel which I preached to you...for I delivered to you as of first importance what I also received, that **Christ died for our sins according to the Scriptures, and that He was buried, and that He was raised on the third day according to the Scriptures**. (1 Corinthians 15:3-4).

Purchase this book at www.amazon.com
Purchase this book at www.buckanderson.com
Free word studies aids at www.buckanderson.com

Made in the USA
Coppell, TX
15 January 2021